THE C-SUITE ⋯⋯⋯ GUIDE FOR
COLLABORATION AND COMMUNICATION

# TALENT
## —— IS A ——
# TEAM SPORT

FIND, ATTRACT,
AND KEEP THE TALENT
YOU NEED TO BE
FUTURE-READY

# DENISE GRAZIANO

*Cover image credit: Shutterstock.*

ISBN-10: 1725022109
ISBN-13: 978-1725022102

# DOWNLOAD THE WORKSHEETS FREE!

## READ THIS FIRST

Just to say thanks for buying my book, I would like to give you the worksheets as a full size PDF 100% free.

## TO DOWNLOAD GO TO:

http://talentisateamsport.com/worksheets

# Table of Contents

# THE PROBLEM

THE
TALENT
SHORTAGE

*Only 38% of companies take a modern approach of building a talent pool for when positions arise.*

—Aberdeen Hiring Tomorrow's Workforce 2018

# Overview

Successful companies do not achieve the ultimate goals of revenue, retention, and repeat business by accident; they do it by design. Wouldn't that be easier if the rules of competition stayed the same? Regardless of industry, employees, customers, and technology are changing the rules and pace of competition. Wayne Gretzky stated it best when he said he skated to where the puck was going next. In many organizations though, this is a challenge because the "puck," or business conditions, are moving faster than leadership can make decisions and faster than organizations move as a whole.

In the context of having the ideal talent in place to give you a competitive advantage, outdated approaches and slow decision making will not only cause companies to lose out on talent, they may lose them to competitors. Leaders work to build a sustainable culture, but it can be destroyed by turnover, losing key employees, and being unable to successfully recruit and hire the key players that will be able to take the company into its next phase of growth.

The cost of doing nothing or doing things the same old way that created the problem to begin with is steep. Lost revenue, as well as diminished productivity and morale directly affect company culture and customer experiences. The high cost of employee and customer turnover creates a negative cycle. This is not a human resources problem. It is a systemic issue that needs the entire C-suite to own their parts of the solution and take consistent action.

The old approach of posting jobs when positions arise, and the slow, methodical interviewing process once considered standard, no longer serves companies, because these processes no longer serve candidates. Candidates want and expect more because they have options.

In this book I want to bridge the gap and present solutions and emerging best practices that enable you to have the personnel to serve clients now, fill your pipeline for long-range plans and help give you a competitive edge in your market. This will take the involvement and effort from of all the C-suite branches. It will take a nimble approach, an open mind, and a reality check, because companies are not in as much control as they believe.

Only 38% of companies take a modern approach to building a talent pool for when positions arise. If you're one of the 62% who have not, you will likely see a pattern in which you will be missing out on the talent you need now and for long-range plans. However, the 38% that have embraced progressive hiring strategies are not fully insulated from talent issues simply by having a larger pool from which to draw. Retention is as important.

Again, this is not a human resources issue. It is a team-oriented leadership mandate. Leaders must evangelize employees to want to be at work because they feel they are making a difference, regardless of the roles they have. Employees naturally want to feel valued and appreciated. This philosophy must emanate from all levels of leadership.

Speed, agility, clarity, and communication are the hallmarks of recruiting that serve today's candidates and companies alike.

# INTRODUCTION

It is time to work together.

The recruitment and retention practices that brought you to this point cannot take you where you need and want to go. Maintaining a competitive edge in your market will require skills, innovation, and a culture that support long-range growth. Finding and keeping the people that fuel success is a concern and top priority for many companies. Yet some still don't understand why they are missing out on great candidates or why they are losing strong employees.

Companies are hiring, and the best employees are in demand. Outdated HR approaches and attitudes will not land them. A shift occurred with customers when they discovered their voice and a powerful ally: social media. Employees have found their power. They ask, "why not?" They want and expect more from employers. Unfortunately for companies, those expectations are fluid, expanding, and publicly shared.

During an address at a leadership event, a CEO of a Fortune 500 company described a recent encounter with a young, new employee. The new hire went up to this CEO and asked him, "what are you and the company going to do to help me advance my career?" Once the chuckles died down in the room, the CEO went on to say that if he had done that 40 years ago at his first job, he likely would have been fired. Times have changed, and the reality is that innovation must start in the C-suite, to get ahead and stay ahead of the competition.

Retaining key talent grows more challenging. Companies strive for diversity and flexibility. Yet they struggle with the new methods required to keep valued players in their organizations. They must nurture and grow those relationships.

Customers, stakeholders, and shareholders expect agility, flexibility, and next-level products and services. Those attributes and more are required of the entire C-suite, who must work together to achieve these outcomes. But silos, and often a lack of support and involvement from senior leadership, exacerbate the talent dilemma.

*Talent is a Team Sport* is a C-level action guide which illustrates and outlines emerging best practices to attract, retain, and grow your talent, and ultimately to increase revenue, retention, and loyalty. This guide is not for companies or executives who feel that the status quo will carry them forward. It is for companies who realize that the cost of doing nothing, or maintaining current practices, will lead to only mediocre results in the future.

I have been fortunate to be a trusted advisor to the C-suite for decades. For more than 30 years I have observed and helped clients build better relationships, both internally with their employees and externally with customers. My priority is helping companies differentiate and gain competitive advantage in their markets, by leveraging the power of positive employee and customer experiences.

Our clients appreciate us for bringing order and clarity to a situation and creating tailored solutions for their challenges. We have helped them communicate effectively with employees to vitalize the workforce and foster brand ambassadorship from the inside of their companies.

How would prospective employees rate your company's candidate recruiting experience? Worse than just losing out on a great employee if the recruiting process is poor, these candidates often leave with a negative opinion of the brand overall.

How would employees, customers, and investors rate your employer brand? Do you have a goal for what that should look like now and in the future? Inconsistencies between your internal and external brand images can hamper your ability to attract best-in-class talent and fill your long-range pipeline.

Companies and high-level leaders often don't realize the challenges and impressions they're presenting to their team members (and customers). Miscommunication, lack of clarity, and feedback that goes unheard, devalued, or is misunderstood can start to disrupt productivity and trust.

This book will help leaders see that their interactions internally with employees and externally with customers could be sabotaging their growth. Additionally, they can discover how to take a silo-free, collaborative approach to securing the resources they need for the future.

With *Talent is a Team Sport,* you will have a strategic action guide showing how leadership roles integrate to:

- Gain visibility in the places that candidates are looking for opportunities, not just where you are posting jobs

- Attract and build a pool of ideal talent

- Keep the valuable employees you have

- Communicate with employees to vitalize the workforce and foster brand ambassadorship from inside your company

- Prepare for the agile needs that enable a company to adapt to marketplace shifts

- Use tools to streamline and accelerate results

- Avoid blind spots and overlooked metrics that matter

Sustained growth and success requires a strategic look at the talent you have and the talent you need to advance, to stay ahead of competitors. For any size organization, building a team of talented players is not solely the responsibility of the human resources department. New rules in this candidate-driven economy demand new collaboration, consistent communication, and a proactive, silo-free approach. While the CEO, CFO, CHRO, and CCO must act strategically together, virtually every other member of the C-suite has a role in securing and keeping the team you need.

Why me? In addition to my history as an executive with over 30 years of helping companies communicate and build better relationships with their employees and clients, I have been a team player all my life. I was a two-sport NCAA Division 1 athlete in college. I have coached successful youth travel sports. In business and sports, I know the importance of stacking your team to create wins.

Why now? Every week I see another study that confirms that recruitment and retention is an urgent challenge facing companies globally. Employee and candidate expectations have grown; they will not decrease, even in an employer-favored market. How you attract and keep your most valuable resources will be the catalyst to future growth. This CEO is ready to help you. Let's all work on it together.

*25% of insurance employees are eligible to retire in 2018. Fewer than 5% of Millennials are interested in insurance careers.*

—Insurance Careers Movement

# How Did We Get Here?

The talent shortage is real and stems from many factors that, even while in plain sight, seems to have crept up on companies. It has been easier to ignore, defer, or reason that recruitment would not become an issue or not make as much of an impact.

For example: In the insurance industry, there is a squeeze from both ends of the age spectrum. In 2018, 25% of the industry are now able to retire. 25%! And reportedly, fewer than 5% of millennials show interest in the industry at all. Insurance executives are now facing challenges by not acknowledging this reality and acting sooner. Yet, of the 25% that may retire, only some of those roles will need replacing. The remaining workforce will be able to fill some of the vacancies, while technology can pick up the slack.

Another contributing factor to the challenge of enlisting new employees is that the insurance industry has a reputation for being stodgy and boring and is often misunderstood. I have often asked my college interns about the companies that come to campus to recruit. Insurers still recruit, but fewer of the students see this as a compelling industry. When I ask the students why, they say that insurance is boring and thus, not interesting to them. As a marketer; I can never resist reframing an image. Technology, cybersecurity, and autonomous driving cannot exist without insurance coverage. Most students say that they would consider the jobs if recruiters appealed to their interests to present the industry in a more exciting way.

Some industry veterans realize the need for a makeover. They have created a foundation to educate and generate interest among new grads. Younger insurance employees have encouraged the industry to modernize for customers and employees. Invigorating the industry's career image requires a joint effort from seasoned and younger executives.

The talent shortage can decrease productivity, service, and overall customer experience. Losing the accumulated knowledge and practical experience as a result of execs retiring poses other problems. Risk assessment for insurance underwriting requires art and science. Machines cannot replicate the nuances and skills that come from experience of what has worked and what has not. Most insurance companies sell similar products and services. Experience is often their differentiator, so retaining experienced top talent matters.

The same can be true for many industries in which competition is tight because the product offerings are so alike. It is the experience of their team that they rely on as a major differentiator. So when companies lose those seasoned employees, perhaps to competitors, they forfeit some of their proclaimed advantage. Attracting and keeping those who make you shine to your customers cannot be presumed as an absolute.

*Globally the talent shortage has reached a 12-year high. 67% of larger companies struggle to fill open jobs.*

—Manpower Group 2018 Talent Shortage Survey

# WHAT WORKED BEFORE IS NOT ENOUGH NOW

Revenue, retention, and repeat business: this is how successful businesses have operated for centuries. While these goals remain the same, the conditions and players in the game are not. Disruption has become the norm, not the exception. Elevated expectations from customers and employees are a struggle for many companies to meet.

The two biggest catalysts for growth and change in virtually any business today are technology and people, both the people that the company serves and those that serve the company. You cannot have a successful company without customers or without innovative and dedicated employees. Even the most basic product or service requires the latest in technology to promote, sell, maintain, and serve, to compete and stay ahead of the competition.

Since customers discovered the impact and reach of a variety of social media platforms, companies have had to change how they operate. Companies now respond, react, treat, and serve customers differently because their expectations are ever-evolving and growing. Speed, delivery, convenience, omnichannel access, and communications necessary to keep up with these demands require technology. But technology cannot create or maintain itself. Companies need the best and brightest talent to manage and develop the technological advances needed to succeed in the future.

Unfortunately, the evergreen supply of ideal employees that companies once relied upon has disappeared. For the first time in recent memory, there are more jobs than there are people to fill them. The most current executive surveys and research studies emphatically concur that talent shortages are a concern and priority for companies and their leaders.

Why is it so hard to find and keep good people now?

Employee expectations have changed and grown as much as those of the customer. Economic and market drivers have changed to create the current candidate-favored conditions. There are fewer workers with the necessary skills. Thus, building the team you need and want for current and future demands has become far more complex. Just as customer expectations will not ebb, neither will those of the employee.

It is critical for companies to focus inward on their employer brand to build the future-ready version of their company.

The reality is that the practices that have carried you and your company to this point are not enough to take you to your next levels of growth, profitability, and long-range goals.

Employees have more options than ever before. In some industries, key talent is in scarce supply and much more difficult to find, let alone employ. And, you must also retain the valuable people that have brought your company to the present-day. Even those who are not necessarily looking for new roles could consider switching jobs (possibly to a competitor). Therefore, protecting the team you have is critical. And recruiting the staff that will strengthen your company now and for the future is equally vital to success.

There are so many variables at play today. When in unfamiliar territory, sometimes the best course of action is to do some introspection and simplify. It will take a collaborative effort from senior leadership to preserve a company's most vital asset, the employees. The new approach must be strategic and unified, where all lanes merge, to steer the company forward. The typical practices where the departmental silos rule and executives simply update each other on their respective progress will not work.

The cost of doing nothing, not adapting to the new business conditions, will not yield the same results as in the past. It will lead to mediocrity or worse. Awareness of having to make changes is not enough. Action is required to elevate your organization to future-ready status.

# TAKEAWAYS

- The evergreen supply of ideal employees has disappeared. Companies must be proactive and creative to attract who they need.

- Employee expectations have changed and grow much like those of the customer. Companies must listen early and take action often.

- Evaluate your employer brand. What do you want it to mean to work for your company? Would employees agree?

- Awareness is not enough. Action is required to prepare and create change for the future.

# MANUFACTURING IS TURNING AWAY BUSINESS DUE TO TALENT SHORTAGES

The good news is that manufacturing is on a major upswing. The bad news: Over 34% of manufacturers have had to turn away business and have subsequently lost revenue because of insufficient talent. More bad news: Employers don't have an immediate remedy, so nearly 67% have been overloading their existing teams to meet demands. This is a temporary fix at best, because it will cause burnout of valuable employees.

A just work harder approach is not sustainable for the long term. Manufacturers are, therefore, attempting other remedies including: scheduling training programs to develop skills, employing temporary workers, and attempting to persuade workers to defer retirement.

The urgent challenge for manufacturers is to keep up with the increasing volume of work, and to that end, they need qualified employees. That said, some manufacturers, including the auto industry, have been facing a talent shortage for many years. Current demands are exacerbating conditions and it is taking a toll. Companies are in a reactive mode.

A number of factors contribute to the shortage, some of which were foreseeable yet were not prepared for. Fewer children were born of the last few generations. Older workers are approaching retirement. Fewer people had been attending trade schools. The skills gap is real, and companies cannot up-skill workers fast enough. Nearly 80% of manufacturers surveyed stated that they have unfilled positions in their organizations.

Nevertheless, hiring candidates that are merely adequate instead of ideal, simply to fill job vacancies, will net poor results.

## SCENARIO

A consultant was assessing a young engineer in charge of a multi-million-dollar piece of equipment that creates expensive manufacturing parts. When asked a basic question about his process, the engineer replied, "the computer just does all that for me." He didn't understand the process, nor did he think that it was necessary. Unfortunately, manufacturers are finding this to be a common trait among young engineers.

Premier companies are frustrated by the new candidate-driven market. Younger applicants who receive substantial job offers fail to respond quickly to the company or ultimately decline the offers. Some organizations are puzzled as to why they are losing employees or prospects, assuming that these candidates are just a "bad fit"; alternatively, these organizations may offer some other excuse that ignores the reality. The old hiring methods that served companies in the past are insufficient to satisfy today's candidates. So, to fill seats, employers may be settling for less than the best additions to their teams.

Manufacturers have noticed new challenges presented by some of the younger hires. They often don't show up on time or they spend too much time with their cell phones during work hours. There is a notable decline in professionalism.

More leadership training is needed. Engineers are promoted to managerial positions but are not always trained to lead. Promotions do not magically bestow managerial or social skills. Thus, those without enough training may abdicate their authority because they don't know how to manage. So, they don't. Poor managers cause employee productivity and engagement to suffer and can drive away good talent.

When asked why they tolerate such unprofessional behavior, some executives say it is easier. They don't want to go through the time or expense of starting over with the job posting, searching, interviewing, hiring, and the onboarding process.

Many companies see the symptoms, but they don't understand that it's their processes that must change. For example, in an overstretched work environment, managers are busy, and the last thing they want to do is write a job description. So, they may ask the last person that had the job to write one, instead of crafting a new one that is more relevant for the role and the skills that are now needed. They may also use a generic description they found online. Or it may get passed off to HR or an outside recruiter who cannot possibly know the manager's needs nor that of the internal team. This will lead back to the unfortunate cycle when employers are finding that too many candidates are a "bad fit."

Manufacturers are trying to change their habits of the past. They are enticing younger workers with more bells and whistles. But they are often missing the mark on what works. They are not viewing their companies through the lens of current candidates. Nor have they presented an employer brand that is enticing to their ideal talent. Installing game rooms and basketball hoops won't do it. Getting in touch with the expectations of their talent pool will.

Another symptom of old behaviors and an overworked team is that the onboarding process is often bare-bones at best. This is indicative of organizations in any industry or at any employee level. "Here's your computer, your work station, handbook…welcome aboard." New hires thrive—and stay—when relationships are nurtured from day one.

Companies are struggling to meet demands, straining the current workforce to keep up, so finding remedies quickly is essential. Retention is of the utmost importance. Nimble, collaborative thinking is the fastest path to solutions for both retention and attraction.

One current example of such creative collaboration is to entice young people to trade schools and other careers. A recent report stated that the new housing market is challenged by the fact that there are not enough young workers to build the homes. Builders that are not meeting demands are losing revenue. Companies in industries that are misunderstood and overlooked by young applicants must do a better job of appealing to their interests as well as presenting opportunities for growth.

Manufacturers, builders and other industries are working with government-led initiatives to create educational programming. By creating a "perfect world" set of employee ideals and targeting high school and college kids, employers can help establish a pipeline for future talent. The Mike Rowe Works Foundation created the Profoundly Disconnected campaign (http://profoundlydisconnected.com) to educate on the critical need to fill the skills gap, alternatives to traditional four year degrees. It offers scholarship opportunities for students who want to enter trade schools.

All of this creative outreach serves the companies' and industries' best interests. Having to promote a career path is a new challenge for some industries. However it is an investment in their future success. In this case collaboration with the government and with competitors may create results faster.

## TAKEAWAYS

- Manufacturers' short term fix of working existing workers harder is not sustainable and will lead to worse shortages.

- Collaboration with government and other organizations to increase interest in trade careers among students is a model other industries should follow.

- Communication and leadership training should be prioritized in manufacturing, as high levels of inconsistency often occur between shifts and disparate locations.

*90% of job seekers say they would be less likely to apply for a job after reading reviews of poor customer or employee treatment.*

—CareerArc Employer Branding Study

# THE COST OF DOING NOTHING: USING GLASSDOOR AND INDEED REVIEWS AS A ROADMAP TO CHANGE

Many companies are seeing HR costs rise because traditional recruitment marketing and retention practices that worked in the past do so no longer. Subsequently, they are losing good employees and candidates.

Instead of implementing modern recruitment and retention methods, companies are making excuses for conditions resulting from the use of obsolete strategies. Some common ones:

- Excuse A: The right candidates did not apply.

  Reality: The company was invisible, confusing, or undesirable. Possible causes were that recruitment marketing failed; the position was not posted in the right places to attract the ideal employee; the description did not really match what the role entailed; the required candidate experience was such that it turned off the prospect even if it were their ideal job; the customer brand did not match the employer brand; the new hire onboarding experience was insufficient, and the candidate reconsidered and left; or the ideal candidates never even applied because of negative online reviews.

- Excuse B: Good employees are leaving.

  Reality: Retention practices fail or do not exist. Employees do not feel valued. They do not feel connected to the company mission. They do not believe or trust in leadership. They receive information on a "need to know" basis, and employees then fill in their own details. Employees provide feedback on areas of concern, but the company does not take action. The company lacks flexibility or adequate compensation and benefits. Infrastructure, tools, and technology are insufficient. As a result, negative customer feedback wears good employees out.

- Excuse C: The candidate could not wait.

  Reality: The process took too long. A colleague at a global advisory firm wanted a specific addition to his team. He had been recruiting this high-potential candidate for months and finally the timing was right. My colleague made the initial offer and the prospect countered. Then, the process slowed: The CFO had to approve the offer; the candidate had other considerations and could wait only so long; the finance department took too long, and they ultimately lost out on this high-powered sales agent. Historically, this company could take its time presenting an offer. Not anymore.

- Excuse D: Employer review sites are portraying the company unfairly.

  Reality: Companies are ignoring warning signs that could save them time, money, and aggravation. The comments are a roadmap to corrective measures.

  Don't ignore the warning signs that suggest negative reviews may be impacting your hiring and retention. You may first notice that your job postings are not getting the number of applications that they used to. Next, you may notice that the quality of the applicants you do get is declining. You may finally get a call from your recruiting firm telling you that applicants are not applying for your positions because of what they read on Glassdoor, Indeed, ZipRecruiter, et al.

  Companies may reason: Yes, there was a restructuring; yes, some good people had to be laid off; yes, we have some managers in a particular location who could use some training; yes, our culture could use a little improvement. Yet, knowing all of this, some companies may still ask of job seekers: Don't you still want to apply here?

We all look for the recommendations of someone who has previous experience before we buy something or make a big decision. It streamlines the process and perhaps protects us from a situation we would be better off avoiding. That is why we look on Amazon for product reviews, Kelley Blue Book or other car resources before buying a car, travel sites before booking a hotel or destination, and Google or Yelp before dining.

Job applicants are no different. They have options and they want to avoid making decisions that they may regret by being uninformed.

Some CEOs tell me that they peek in one of these posting sites periodically to see what people are saying. These are usually the ones that have good reviews and good ratings. Why is that? Because they know what it takes to keep good employees, and they want to be sure they do not miss any red flags that may need intervention.

For some executives, they view these sites as a thorn in the side, full of anonymous critics and disgruntled former employees. Some of that may be true. But just as you can sense a "hater" on Yelp or TripAdvisor, you can also identify those on a recruiting site.

The alarm should sound for companies when they see trends and patterns, especially those regarding trust and leadership. These job site reviews offer a veritable gold mine of free insight into potential employee churn triggers and applicant repellents. Companies can gain perspective. They may see how a particular event was mishandled in the eyes of the employees; they may be able to identify poor conduct, a lack of communication, or myriad other factors that have negatively impacted employees.

When patterns emerge, such as complaints about a particular location, management, communication, changes in benefits, or declines in morale and culture overall, it is an opportunity for companies to investigate and take corrective action.

It is not a time, however, to hide the reviews or hide from the reviews. This is an increasingly frequent impulse for companies: the desire to remove the reviews or suppress them. Generally speaking, reviews cannot be removed or altered, especially if they are anonymous. Some companies try to suppress them by driving the search results farther down on the page, and replace them with positive articles, news, or comments. While that may help in overall search results, the reviews will still exist on the job search sites. Applicants actively search for reviews, and 90% of them will avoid applying if they don't like what they are reading.

Take action, don't "take cover."

Look for patterns in the comments. Respond to comments that warrant a reply. However, too many companies do this in such a way that comes across as disingenuous. As much as prospects read reviews, they look to find if and how companies respond.

When patterns such as distrust or miscommunication from leadership emerge, swift action is needed to prevent future damage. Gain additional insight from employees to determine the causes. There are myriad tools to survey, communicate, assess, and create data points. Initiate corrective measures. Erosion in trust will both repel candidates and drive additional employees away.

If particular locations are identified as having problems, investigate and make adjustments accordingly. In all cases, these comments are direct insight to matters that should be addressed and at the very least monitored.

## TAKEAWAYS

- Companies are making excuses for obsolete strategies.

- Take online reviews seriously. Take action, do not try to hide them or hide from them.

- Look for patterns and trends in the comments and use them to take swift action when needed.

- Red flags to watch for include comments about leadership, trust or communication

- Respond with care to negative comments that warrant one. Take care not to seem flippant or disingenuous with responses.

# THE COST OF DOING NOTHING: A LEGAL POINT OF VIEW

It is not simply HR costs that are rising; it is legal costs, too. This stems from poor communication, poor company culture, or a damaged employer brand; this may also stem from a lack of emotional intelligence from managers. For example there was an instance in which an employee had to file a worker's comp claim with her manager after suffering an injury on the job. The incident was well documented, and this person had never filed a claim before. The manager did not respond compassionately to the situation; instead, he made a sarcastic and derogatory comment. A routine claim became a much costlier issue because of the lack of emotional intelligence of the manager.

How a situation is handled initially can either cause it to be settled reasonably and amicably or cause the matter to escalate. This inflates the cost of the settlement and legal fees, and it negatively impacts morale as well. If made public, a negative scenario may repel potential candidates. Depending on the severity, it may drive away good employees or require crisis communication to contain the matter. This can also negatively impact customer and investor relations.

General Counsel handles matters that often show a pattern of costly behaviors. These behaviors might be related to a host of situations, including sexual harassment, ageism, lack of emotional intelligence, insufficient training, or accidents. Any of them could cost the company an extraordinary sum. If the legal department sees patterns in any one area, there is certainly a need for corrective action. And by taking a proactive approach, the GC can work with other officers of the company to mitigate future issues.

In another instance, a service company's legal department was looking for a resource to "clean up and bury" some poor reviews that former employees had posted about the employer. They were looking for a positive PR campaign to help cover up the negative posts or drive them much farther down in the search results list.

This effort would have essentially resulted in putting lipstick on the proverbial pig. Patterns of negative reviews are indicative of problems that need correcting, not concealing. On reviewing the comments, it was clear that there were leadership concerns and conditions at the company that no amount of cosmetic treatments could alter. No company wants to admit they have internal issues. However, HR risks in today's workplace cannot be ignored.

Sexual harassment claims are increasing. Situations vary greatly, from the inappropriate comments to the more serious physical assaults. Employment attorneys routinely see cases in which a suggestive remark, which may have been tolerated in years past, is no longer acceptable.

Ageism claims are also costing companies a great deal. Comments that are meant in jest, are considered stereotypical, or are thinly disguised as insinuations that an employee is old, are unacceptable in the workplace. They are also fuel for potentially costly legal battles and image problems.

At the most basic level, companies should have an established and enforced code of behavior. For cases that escalate and result in the termination of an employee, there are additional internal costs that include the expense of replacing the employee, as well as the subsequent loss of productivity, morale, and potential client impact.

The cost of doing nothing can be staggering. A $10,000 claim can balloon to $500K in legal costs alone for an entry-level employee in a sexual harassment case. With senior employees, those costs can inflate exponentially. If the conditions and behaviors are pervasive in the company, those costs multiply, possibly to a debilitating level. Outside the company, if public image damage becomes magnified, customers and prospects alike could be driven away.

Seemingly unconnected problems share a common solution: collaboration vs siloing. Changing behaviors requires the input and collaboration of many areas of leadership. For example, the General Counsel is a key to illuminating the areas that must change. Human resources must inform and establish policies. Communications can help ensure that messaging is relevant and "sticks" with employees. The CIO facilitates the delivery of the message via company infrastructure. Leaders from all domains must a) support these changes, b) lead by example, and c) enforce policies. Working together toward such solutions can save companies untold sums.

## TAKEAWAYS:

- The legal department is a key to preventing unnecessary costs by illuminating behaviors that must be changed.

- Working in tandem with HR, Communication, CIO, Learning & Development, Legal can help create policies, programming and codes of behavior where they are in need of reinforcement.

*87% of companies cannot easily maintain their talent pipeline.*

—Aberdeen

# ADAPT, DON'T ABANDON

If you are one of the small percentage of companies that have figured out how to keep the valued talent you have, and how to find and attract the people with the skills you need to grow, then guard your secret approach carefully, because that is your new competitive advantage.

Businesses are in unfamiliar territory. For the first time in recent memory, there are more job openings then there are people. Let that sink in. Companies wonder why their offers are going unaccepted—industry giants who in the past simply made a job offer and would expect it to be readily accepted on the merits of the company name alone. Things have changed. Right now, and for the foreseeable future, it is a candidate's market. Beyond that, the ratio of jobs and candidates may fluctuate, but the expectations of candidates are forever changed.

The model of finding talent as roles need to be filled is ineffective, especially when the pool of applicants is small.

Establishing a pipeline for future roles, including succession planning, is essential to being future ready.

Companies using the old model and methods are losing ideal candidates to competitors. Worse than that, companies are also losing valued team members to competitors that are creating a pool of candidates for their future needs. That is why retention as a proactive approach is critical for success now and for the future.

If you're like most of the 87% of companies and executives that have difficulty maintaining a talent pipeline (Aberdeen), you should be concerned. You are likely losing people, clients, and market share, but even worse, you are in a poor position to achieve your 10-year growth plans as a result.

It is time to act and develop processes that adapt to the new talent realities, but do not abandon all your current business practices or people that have gotten you to this point in your trajectory.

Like it or not, your customers and employees have the power to derail your plans and your success. Am I overstating? It depends on who you ask:

- Do you think that Snapchat imagined they could lose $1.6 billion of market share value in one day because of one celebrity tweet? This influencer no longer wanted to use the platform. The comment exposed the fact that Snapchat neglected to communicate with their customers before rolling out sweeping platform changes.

- Do you think that Wells Fargo could have envisioned the lawsuits, negative publicity, and challenges that stemmed from policies, leadership behaviors, and employees who opened accounts without client consent?

- Do you think that United Airlines could have anticipated the legal, financial, and brand costs associated with a series of incidents that exposed culture and leadership liabilities?

But it does not have to be a single, devastating event that derails a company. A pattern of small, isolated, and insignificant client-impacting instances can generate negative reviews, a poor brand image, and reduced revenue. Ninety-two percent of customers will switch brands after fewer than 3 bad experiences. And it can impact your ability to attract ideal talent in the future.

Today's candidates want to associate and work for a socially responsible brand, one that treats customers well. Before making a purchase, both B2B and B2C customers do their own research, read reviews, and solicit peer recommendations prior to reaching out for sales help. Candidates today do the same type of research before deciding if they would work for a company.

Candidates consider brand image. Poor client experiences, whether they are due to a lack of ideal talent, poor training, or any number of reasons, color the opinions of prospective employees and customers alike. If a brand does not align with candidate expectations, they reject the company as an employer, and possibly as a customer, too. And…they will share their experiences with friends.

Millennials are now the largest segment of the workforce. They are the first generation to grow up with technology, and most share their lives in real time. Companies must realize that poor recruiting and hiring practices are also shared. When bad candidate experiences are exposed, they repel good candidates and employees. Companies struggling to maintain a pipeline cannot afford such mistakes.

## TAKEAWAYS

- Maintaining a talent pipeline is a competitive advantage, and key to achieving 10 year growth plans.

- The ratio of jobs and candidates may fluctuate, but the expectations of candidates are forever changed.

- Retention as a proactive approach is critical for success now and for the future.

- Poor customer experiences can deter potential candidates.

- Poor candidate experiences can cause them to reject the company as a customer too.

- Today's younger workforce shares their experiences, good or bad, and it impacts a company's ability to recruit.

# SECTION TWO
## THE SOLUTION
### SURROUNDING THE PROBLEM

*In the U.S., the average trust in institutions declined to only 45% trust (down from 68% in 2017).*

—2018 Edelman Global Trust Barometer

# TRUST: THE FOUNDATION OF ANY RELATIONSHIP

Trust is the foundation for building and keeping a winning team. Trust must first be earned and then maintained. It is not a set-it-and-forget-it personality trait. This applies equally among individuals, employers, and institutions. Leaders must earn the trust of their employees or risk losing those relationships. Open and transparent communication, even in difficult times, is a must. When employee surveys reveal a decline of trust in leadership, it usually stems from poor or absent communication.

Any size company, from small to global, can make false assumptions when they fail to monitor and nurture employee relationships. When employees become disengaged from leadership, it leads to fear and distrust, which negatively impacts productivity, customer experience, and morale. Disengaged employees cost employers billions of dollars annually. Conversely, engaged employees are five times more likely to recommend their companies to others, four times more likely to do something good beyond that which is expected, three times more likely to work late, and five times more likely to suggest improvements at work (Temkin).

In their Trust Barometer, Edelman found that 52% of people view employees as "credible" or "very credible" sources of information about a company. When employees are uninformed or misinformed by leadership, that credibility affects client relationships as a result.

Companies should not treat employees with a need-to-know-basis approach; otherwise, the staff is likely to fill in the blanks with their own details. Leadership must ensure that all levels of management provide a consistent message, so that information is not received differently across departments, locations, or shifts. Especially when difficult news must be shared, leaders must demonstrate trust in their employees and in their relationships by communicating a unifying message. Changing behavior cannot occur without trust. And trust goes both ways.

A CEO noticed that she rarely got any pushback from her senior team. She had the wisdom and foresight to question whether her leadership was indisputable or if there was a communication problem. After a pattern of this acquiescence, she decided to test her theory. She decided to make a phony avant-garde proposal that should warrant objections and exposition. During the next meeting of her senior team, she rolled out plans for a high-risk, new vertical. Instead of skepticism and questions from these officers, she received plaudits.

Needless to say, this was the catalyst for bringing in a new leadership team. Two takeaways: 1) Leaders should challenge each other and work together to drive the company forward. 2) Trust is a two-way relationship.

Employees need to be able to trust leadership to be authentic, transparent, and guide their company toward success. And leaders need to be able to trust that their employees, no matter how senior, are committed to the good, and the mission, of the company.

Honest communication fosters trust. Solid trust deepens relationships and facilitates growth. A lack of trust erodes relationships and causes a decline in morale and productivity. Driving away good people can become a brand image issue, especially when employees are viewed as credible sources about businesses. The cycle will repeat itself without corrective action.

Taking control, especially if there are trust or communication issues, requires visible, decisive action from leadership. It must become a set the example philosophy, not a set-it-and-forget-it approach. Earn trust consistently.

## TAKEAWAYS:

- Open and transparent communication, even in difficult times, is a must.

- When employee surveys reveal a decline of trust in leadership, it usually stems from poor or absent communication.

- Changing behavior cannot occur without trust.

*Companies that connect employee purpose to company mission outperform competitors by 42%*

—DDI Global Leadership Forecast 2018

## PICC WINNING FRAMEWORK: PASSION MUST BE TIED TO MISSION AND PURPOSE

In 2009 Jack Welch wrote a book called *Winning*. In the book, he explained how everyone wants to win, but not everyone knows how. And I love the powerful simplicity of that truth. Because if winning were clear or easy, anyone could do it, and in all likelihood, everyone *would* do it. In effect, there would be no competition. But we know that the competition for customers, market share, top talent, and investors are fiercer than they have ever been. So, finding and showcasing the differentiator(s) that set you apart and create a competitive advantage are more vital to long-term success than ever before. But you must think like a competitor.

I have been a team player for as long as I can remember. And competing in team sports was one of the best things that I have ever done for myself. I draw upon some of the disciplines that I learned on the volleyball court or on the softball field to this day. It's interesting that to be a successful team player, you must also be a strong individual player. Whether in the athletic world or in the corporate world, teams need a roster of talented individuals with the specific skills needed to serve the organization as a whole.

In my life as an athlete, and over 30 years of working with companies, I see commonalities that create a competitive edge. The PICC Winning framework is simply a frame within which you can create conditions for success, and it is also a reminder for when there is a disconnect from goals and outcomes. This framework is equally effective in sports and in business. But there is an added component required for business success, and that is communication. Used as a guide, the framework impacts revenue, retention, and loyalty for employees and customers, and it is deceptively simple, much like wanting to win but not knowing how to win.

In the next few chapters, I will highlight each component and illustrate how it helps create wins in business. This is not "nice to have" information; it is numbers driven and of significant value to any business industry. PICC stands for Passion, Insight, Commitment, and Communication. Parts of this framework will be discussed out of sequence intentionally for illustrative purposes. The final element of this framework—communication—is the thread that holds this all together, much like communication is essential to the success of the collaboration I stress throughout this book, to solve today's talent challenges.

## PART ONE IS PASSION.

You cannot dominate your market without a passion for your products, your services, and your customers. You might have successes, but you will not dominate the market without passion. Here is the key:

The passion cannot be yours alone. Leaders must communicate and share their passions throughout management levels and through their entire organizations. Your employees are your front line to your customers, and ultimately, to revenue and loyalty.

At the end of the work day, we all have a natural inclination to want to make a difference and contribute with our work. Employees with an emotional connection to their work are more productive. Companies that connect purpose to their mission statement outperformed competitors by 42% (Global Leadership Forecast 2018). They had greater employee engagement and more loyal customers.

Has your mission statement become, or has it always been simply words on a wall instead of a philosophy embraced by employees? Is it merely a statement with no genuine mission, vision, or purpose?

If your employees do not understand their roles in the company mission or feel valued in the company's success, it is not their fault. It is likely that company communications, from leadership and throughout the organization, do not adequately connect with employees and draw them into the company narrative.

When passion and purpose are communicated and conveyed effectively from senior leadership management levels and into the organization, employees feel more compelled to consistently deliver a superior product, service, and customer experience. Stating your mission once is not enough. Vitalize the mission with actions and words.

I love great sports movies, especially the ones with motivational speeches. In *Any Given Sunday*, Al Pacino plays a crusty, older football coach. On a particular game day, he is in the locker room giving an impassioned speech about teamwork and about winning. He tells the players that football is a game of inches, that they all live and die by gaining the inches that are all around them on the field. But it takes teamwork to win. He continues with his speech and then the team roars out on the field toward victory.

Let's put the movie script aside. Are your employees clear on their roles in the company's success? Would your revenue increase if you had a team that was figuratively ready to run out onto the field for you every day? Could your organization outperform your competitors by 42%?

Connecting your company mission to the employee's purpose does not require actors, hall-of-fame coaches, or motivational speeches. It is an attitude that leaders must communicate consistently, though. Identify the mission, and clearly, authentically tell the employees that they are the keys to the company's success. Managers should reinforce this with their direct reports. Company materials amplify the mission and connect employees to it.

*Fortune* magazine profiled the 10 best manufacturing companies to work for. The common denominator for most of them was that their people were the focus of their websites. Employees who are passionate about their work resonate with customers. People want to know that their work is valued, and that what they do matters, regardless of their station in the company. Corporate success is a team effort that begins with passion.

## TAKEAWAYS

- Everyone wants to win, but not everyone knows how (Jack Welch) is a powerfully simple concept. Finding & showcasing the differentiators that set you apart from your competition is more vital than ever.

- Companies that tied purpose to mission outperformed competitors by 42%

- Is your team ready to "run out onto the field" for you daily to deliver on your mission?

- Leadership must maintain a contagious attitude if they want the employees to follow.

- Identify the mission, and clearly, authentically tell the employees that they are the keys to the company's success.

# PICC WINNING FRAMEWORK:
# COMMITMENT

In sports, passion is necessary to win a national championship, to win a gold medal, or to achieve any high honor. Why? Because it takes a lot of work and dedication to realize success at these levels. That dedication—that commitment and follow through—is necessary to win. In sports, that means getting up and training while everybody else is asleep. It means making sacrifices, perhaps missing out on personal events because you must train, travel, or compete. It means doing muscle memory drills until you are so bored and so tired that you can't imagine doing one more. (Muscle memory drills are a coach favorite. You repeat a sequence of motions over and over, until your muscles remember them; the actions become instinctive). But then game day comes, and everything comes together, seemingly without effort. I used to love game days after a string of hard volleyball or softball practices in college. Those drills made game days easy.

In business, those muscle memory drills are the best practices, exercises, assessments, customer avatars, employee avatars, that companies and execs should use to monitor and communicate with clients on an ongoing basis. But so many companies and executives push them aside. Other companies may agree that avatars, assessments, and consistent communication are good ideas, but they don't have the budget for them, so they don't act.

The riskiest position though, comes when companies claim they know what's going on with their clients or with their employees... until they realize that they don't.

I was having lunch with a CMO of a global company, and he said, "may I ask you an HR question?" He went on to share that their HR department had done an annual survey, and the results were bad (The word "annual" is part of the problem). The employees stated that they didn't trust leadership. They didn't see leaders come out of their offices and interact with them, so they didn't feel aligned with the same goals, or in some cases, they didn't feel like they were working at the same company.

Trust issues do not happen overnight. They happen over time. They are a serious red flag of underlying and overt communication issues. They provide an example of what can happen when companies falsely assume that they know what is going on, either outside of the organization with their customers or inside with their employees.

You can have all the passion in the world, but without the commitment part of the framework, it is basically a wish. And you can have all the passion and the commitment in the world, but without the third part of the framework, you are not going to gain a competitive advantage. And I believe this is the most difficult one to get right: Insight.

## TAKEAWAYS

- Trust issues between employees and management do not happen overnight. They happen over time.

- It is essential to keep an open dialogue with employees by surveying them early and often. The days of lengthy annual surveys should be replaced by shorter, more frequent ones.

*Nearly 50% of CEOs are concerned about the data upon which they make decisions.*

—KPMG U.S. CEO Outlook 2017

# PICC WINNING FRAMEWORK:
# INSIGHT

Insight in business comes in so many forms. As leaders, we provide insight. The senior execs and people that we hire, the tools and technology we use, and the advisers and consultants that we retain all provide insight. The key is to ensure that the multifaceted acumen aligns with the true problem at hand. If the two segments misalign, or if the alignment is based upon data that is not monitoring the metrics that you need, the results will not be successful.

## SCENARIO—CASE STUDY OF APPLYING THE PASSION—INSIGHT—COMMITMENT—COMMUNICATION FRAMEWORK

A company's headquarters and flagship location had been thriving for 15 years in an upscale city. Several other offices had been opened since. The most recent one seemed on paper to mimic the demographic of the successful HQ location. But a year later, the new facility was failing; workers were being laid off, and there was little or no market traction. Something was misaligned.

## OUR PROCESS: ASSESS—ACT—CREATE CHANGE

**Assess** the situation from overt and obscure angles to find solutions.

We found that the passion and company message had become diluted and disconnected over the years from the founders' original intentions. Our market research benchmarked them against local and market competitors. Focus groups with a cross section of satisfied customers provided extremely valuable insight. The clients were extraordinarily happy, but they found it difficult to refer business. The customers could not explain the value to cost differentiation in relatable language. The service was superior and costlier but misunderstood and thus lumped into in a broader, general category. The company's marketing and sales materials were confusing for prospects. The value provided was unclear, and the construction inconvenienced readers; subsequently, the materials did not attract customers.

## Act

We rewrote the messaging for new sales collateral and the website, creating a clear, results-oriented message that attracted clients, instead of repelling them. The technicians were neither comfortable nor successful in their dual sales roles. Our sales training reframed their thinking about the sales process. We provided them with more natural language to use with customers. Referrals and upselling increased afterward. Finally, we created a strategic plan to give them visibility and traction in the market. We realigned the company's outreach to the correct demographic. The company leaders were able to build key relationships in that high-value region. By introducing the leaders to joint venture partners, they rapidly elevated their profile.

## Create Change

The Result: One year later the company hosted a grand reopening in that space. The facility had more than doubled in size to accommodate the growth from the changes and course correction.

### SUMMARY OF APPLYING THE PASSION—INSIGHT— COMMITMENT—COMMUNICATION FRAMEWORK:

Company leaders rediscovered their passion and tied mission to purpose with the staff. They sought and applied the insight necessary to create change. The company committed to executing the steps over the months that followed. This new outreach helped build relationships with ideal centers of influence. Throughout the process, they communicated the new results-driven messaging. They did this both internally with employees and externally with prospects and customers.

Decisions based on flawed data or from an incomplete perspective slow progress. Select the right combination of data, metrics, and insight for the challenge at hand. A multi-faceted approach is more effective than using a singular viewpoint.

## TAKEAWAYS

The PICC Winning framework is simply that, a frame within you can create conditions for success, and a reminder for when there is a disconnect from goals and outcomes.

**Passion** for what you do (mission) and who you do it for (purpose) as a company is contagious. The absence of passion is equally contagious. What winners do you know of that lacked passion? Identify the mission, and clearly, authentically tell the employees that they are the keys to the company's success.

**Insight** for the situation at hand is critical. While that seems obvious, the fact that 50% of CEOs are concerned about the data upon which they make decisions speaks to the need for soliciting the ideal insight for the situation.

**Commitment** is the follow through that makes any plan a reality. Much like diets, projects and goals that go unfinished, the culprit is usually a lack of commitment. Collaboration it is essential to keep the levels of commitment consistent with all parties, both leaders and employees. When "surrounding" this talent problem with a team approach, accountability is an essential and natural element.

**Communication** in business is the key to all of the above being conveyed clearly, consistently and authentically to all stakeholders involved to achieve goals and "wins."

# CHANGING BEHAVIORS

Changing behaviors is a common and frequent need in business. New initiatives, updated policies, upgrades to infrastructure, compliance issues, and correcting unacceptable conduct: All of these actions and more demand that we change our behaviors. No one likes change, especially forced or sweeping ones, even if they are for the good of the enterprise (as well as our own good). But what if you could more readily *inspire* change?

## SCENARIO

Imagine a disheveled looking blind man sitting on a cardboard box in the middle of a busy metropolitan plaza. He has a handwritten sign on a smaller piece of cardboard that reads, "I'm blind, please help." People walk hurriedly by him on their way to work, lunch, or wherever. Occasionally you notice the plunk of a few coins onto his mat. Then a business woman wearing heels walks by, pauses in front of the man, and picks up his sign. Without a word, she takes out a pen and writes a new message on the other side of his cardboard. The man feels her feet and shoes as she does this. She puts the sign down and clicks away in her heels.

In a matter of minutes, the blind man begins to hear a flurry of coins being dropped in front of his new sign, and he eagerly scoops the money closer to him. Hours later, the woman walks by again; he knows it's her by the sound of her walk. She stops, he feels her shoes again, and he asks, "what did you do to my sign?" She replies, "I wrote the same, but in different words." She walks away. The man remains with the sign in front of him, which now reads: "It's a beautiful day and I can't see it."

That scene is from a video published by Andrea Gardner called the Power of Words, which can be found online.

What behaviors could you change with greater and lasting success if only you communicated in such a way to connect emotionally with your intended audience? Adapting to new policies is often easier if we know why a change is made in the first place. Yet so many companies fail when implementing changes because they don't take the time to consider how the message will be received. The "because I'm the boss" approach may be easier for leaders, but they will not secure any fans or ambassadors to help speed the changes along or ensure their success.

For large initiatives, a communications campaign approach is necessary. But for smaller ones, sometimes it comes down to a relatable message. Managers and leaders are busy and do not necessarily have the time to be creative. But there are tools available that can help make messages stick when they are delivered in a relatable or memorable way. For example, many companies and executives successfully use subscription services for movie and audio clips, or memes that tie to a concept or intended change. For example if your sales theme of the week is perseverance, and you tie it to a favorite movie clip, employees will connect better with it.

Granted, some changes are significant and need more care and reinforcement or an orchestrated campaign. Those require consistent communication from leadership. As well, incentives, intersquad competitions, and gamification are all useful tools to inspire and create change.

## ACTION STEPS

- Identify the goal and what needs to change to achieve it.

- Gain leadership buy-in across the enterprise and individual departments as it applies.

- Leadership must set the example. Caution: When leaders take set-it-and-forget-it approaches, or if they feel that a single statement or announcement will suffice to change behaviors, their efforts cannot succeed. How can you expect employees to follow leads that fizzle?

- Set the conditions and provide the tools and technology that help create new behaviors.

- Reward early adopters to entice more ambassadors.

- Consider the message, impact, and perspective of the receivers: M-I-P

  → **Message:** The information to be shared about the situation

  → **Impact:** The intended outcome from sharing the message... What is the goal?

  → **Perspective:** Anticipate how the message will be received in its current form. If it could be negatively perceived, repeat the process to proactively address any objections.

- Consider the receiver's perspective and connect that to the common goal for better outcomes.

*56% of employers globally say written and verbal communication skills are the most valued human strengths. Next are collaboration and problem solving.*

—Manpower Group 2018 Talent Shortage Survey

# COMMUNICATION AND LEADERSHIP

LinkedIn reviewed the backgrounds of 12,000 global CEOs and found that by far, their top field of study was computer science; next were economics and business. It is not surprising then that CEOs may not always be the best communicators. While some leaders find that communication comes easy to them, for others, the skill is one that does not come naturally and has not been nurtured. For businesses to realize an improved level of success—regardless of industry—an increased emphasis must be placed on soft skills, particularly communication.

A colleague of mine who is a psychologist specializes in working with introverted CEOs and other leaders. Her clients—many from the technology industry—are brilliant. But often they lack the social and interpersonal skills that enable them to build relationships with their teams. Their awkwardness is misconstrued as cold, standoffish, and out of touch. These executives seek her help because they struggle with leading meetings, their productivity is not optimal, and they have high turnover.

Not all leaders are born communicators. They must work at it to build relationships with the people they have hired to follow their lead and achieve company goals. Even in a large enterprise where employees may never meet the CEO, employees must have an allegiance and feel a connection to both the company and the leadership. As with any relationship, this must be nurtured, if they intend to keep their employees. Deferring to the communications department to issue statements does not build employee rapport. A better approach is to collaborate with communications departments, to create a philosophy that builds on connecting mission to purpose.

There are tools that leaders can use internally to make their messages stick. Some senior executives seek media training or speaker training, so they can more effectively deliver remarks to investors, customers, employees, or the media. Authenticity is key to delivering messages successfully, even those that are prepared by others.

And if most employers value communication skills, as suggested in the global talent survey by Manpower noted above, leaders must also elevate their skills where needed. How do you know if you need to make changes? Few subordinates will give a senior leader honest feedback. Look at the current commentary from your key stakeholders, especially from employees.

What do internal employee surveys say? If they are not delivered regularly, change that policy and seek feedback in a more frequent and fluid manner. There are tools and apps that make feedback far less cumbersome than lengthy surveys. Agility and speed are necessary to contain potential problems.

Externally, if social media employer sites have negative or diminishing reviews of leadership, examine them for patterns and target areas that need action. Assess why and when those comments began. What changes could have caused the decline? Remember that these are public comments that are potentially deterring qualified applicants and investors.

Customer commentary is also important to heed in the aggregate. In times of crisis, when CEOs do not respond quickly or authentically, negativity goes viral. This, too, impacts other stakeholders. Leaders that are proactive with announcements, whether positive or negative, improve image and are seen as more transparent.

Individual negative views will always exist. However, if there is an overall opinion that needs corrective action, do not dismiss it. It is concerning how many times I hear from department heads that senior leadership disregard troublesome findings or do not acknowledge that there is an issue. Instead, they dismiss the comments and insist: "We don't have a communication problem." Whether from employees or customers, eventually the comments become public via social media. Unfortunately, it is these companies that eventually struggle with turnover and hiring challenges.

In a tight talent market, leaders must take notice of red flags. Stronger communication is a relatively easy corrective measure with lasting results.

## TAKEAWAYS

- Your employees want you to succeed. They want to be led by someone who inspires them and believes in the company mission.

- Remember to consider how your messages, both verbal and non-verbal are being received.

- If your employees' perception differs from your intent, respect that and take action to adjust your communication style and delivery for better outcomes.

*95% of C-suite execs are planning a redesign, with a focus on increasing productivity, yet only 21% see themselves as "change agile."*

—Mercer 2018 Global Talent Trends Report

## COMMUNICATION: THE 4TH PART OF THE COLLABORATION CORE

Goals for change initiatives, reorganization, talent redeployment, or cultural reforms cannot be successful without a compelling narrative. Which professional skill is highly overlooked, underrated, often treated as an afterthought, yet is as vital as fuel for any vehicle on a company's road to success? Clear, consistent, authentic communication.

Each year CEOs and companies set strategic plans to address their top concerns, yet only the most successful prioritize communication as part of their plans. That is why the Chief Communications Officer must be the 4th part of the collaboration core, working in tandem with the CEO, CFO, and CHRO. Having a consistent, cohesive voice that orchestrates all other internal and external messages of a company fuels success.

There is a joke about an older goldfish swimming in a lake and happens to meet two younger goldfish. The older fish greets the younger ones, saying, "good morning boys, how's the water today?" They pass, and after a moment, one of the young fish says to his friend, "what the heck is water?" Communication in business is a lot like water is to those fish: It is overlooked, invisible, and yet vital.

Depending on how it is used, communication is woven into the success or failure of any initiative. It is the story that presents a case, inspires people to act, or explains why something occurred. Regularly though, it is treated as a delivery method instead of as a strategic tool.

Companies spend far too much of their time focusing on customer communications than they do on communicating with their employees. Ninety-five percent of C-level executives are planning a redesign in the next year and want to focus on increasing productivity. Productivity increases, changes in policy, and attempts to build morale need more than a single statement. Communication is a strategic tool, thus the CCO must be an integral part of planning.

Too many times I hear from companies about major plans, and the last component they consider, if at all, is how or when the message will be delivered. Companies spend far more time on marketing than on using dialogue to build relationships. Very often, proactive statements could mitigate the need for crisis communication.

Strong communication is the remedy for many common revenue leaks:

## LOSING EMPLOYEES OR MISSING OUT ON TOP CANDIDATES

Employees are a company's most precious asset and should be treated as such. Engaged employees look beyond the paycheck; they want to know the role they play in a company's success. According to Mercer's Global Talent Trends 2018 Study, 97% of employees value being recognized and rewarded for a wider range of contributions.

CEOs are concerned about the availability of key skills, yet not enough companies market to prospects as they would to customers. Retaining valued employees requires attention and effort that goes far beyond providing benefits, pay, and bonuses.

Fortune 500 companies that excel at recruitment marketing strategies have 62% higher average revenue per year than those with average scores, and 152% higher average revenue per year than those with failing recruitment scores (Smash-Fly's Fortune 500 Report: 2018 Recruitment Marketing Benchmarks).

Attracting today's top talent requires being visible to your prospects, not waiting for them to discover your job posts. It means being transparent, telling stories verbally and visually that convey the internal brand experience. It means being responsive to reviews on Glassdoor or Indeed.

Retaining valued people requires ongoing engagement, employing a multifaceted approach, dictated by the culture of an organization. What remains constant is the need for companies to articulate the path of their organizations and their employees' roles in them. Leaders cannot "set it and forget it" and pass this off to communications or HR departments; leaders must set the example.

## NEGATIVE CUSTOMER REVIEWS OR FEEDBACK

If a pattern of negative customer reviews emerges from direct customer contact, or worse, publicly via social media channels, swift action is needed. The causes can stem from a variety of missed opportunities to keep customers informed. For example, it may be that they are not adequately notified about upcoming changes that will affect them. Or company responses to customer feedback about product quality, service, or experience may not be swift enough to retain customers. Yet, even when companies do prepare customers for change, as did L.L.Bean with their change to a longstanding return policy, they must expect outrage and have a plan to address concerns.

Companies should seek input and insights from client-facing employees about the state of customer relationships. Having this insight before a situation can erupt publicly is invaluable. Empowering customer service employees to resolve problems in real time can help contain potential problems. Training employees to listen to customers, acknowledge problems, and take corrective steps can de-escalate volatile situations. Certainly, when planning significant product or service changes, consider the impact before taking action. When announcing any news, be authentic, provide details, and prepare for potential backlash.

## LOSS OF CUSTOMERS AFTER DIFFICULT NEWS OR A CRISIS

Changes in customer policies, unethical developments, customer breaches, et al, have caused clients to exit, or threaten to do so, en masse, which can have a devastating financial impact on a business.

Long-standing customer policy changes should be announced well in advance of the changes, so that customers do not suspect or imply a cover-up or poor business practices. Unexpected negative developments or crises that are not promptly addressed by leadership can escalate into viral social media issues.

Stock losses, negative press, fines, lawsuits, and damaged customer relationships are possible. For example, United Airlines suffered a 4% decrease in market share after the airline's overbooking practices precipitated a passenger being dragged off a flight. The 2016 Wells Fargo scandal for the unauthorized opening of client accounts resulted not only in penalties but in stock declines and lawsuits.

Difficult news is just that. But, to keep valued employees or customers, a proactive, honest explanation will often stem the tide of a mass exodus for matters to do with price increases, product changes, layoffs, closures, et al. In a crisis situation, however, swift, honest acknowledgement of the problem and a plan for corrective measures is essential to salvaging your business's reputation, as well as employee and customer relationships. Delayed responses escalate, infuriate, and drive stakeholders away.

Companies must remember that communication is a dialogue, not a monologue. Technology gives employees' and customers' voices unprecedented power to impact revenue, retention, and loyalty.

Ongoing communication is the key to any healthy, successful personal relationship. Employee and customer relationships also need communication to thrive, perhaps more than ever in our hyper-connected environment. For any plan, convey your intentions succinctly and deliberately, to avoid potential missteps along the way. Lead with communication.

## TAKEAWAYS

- Goals for change initiatives, reorganization, talent redeployment, or cultural reforms cannot be successful without a compelling narrative.

- Communication must be viewed as a strategic tool, not simply a delivery method. Rely on the CCO as an integral part of planning and execution to find, attract, and retain talent.

- Be visible to your ideal talent where they are, not just where you post jobs. Tell stories that draw them into your brand experience. Engage with them to create a warm pool of talent.

- Communication is a dialogue, not a monologue. Do not discount the power that employees and customers have to impact revenue, retention, and loyalty.

# THE COST OF THINKING COMMUNICATION DOES NOT MATTER:
## CASE STUDY EXAMPLES

Here are two cautionary case studies for leaders who do not think that an investment in recruiting and retention communication matters.

**A global financial company whose employees mistrust leadership:** In which multiple CxOs step down, leave, are replaced... And then so are the replacements, because the root of the issue was not corrected.

- Market leading company conducts annual employee survey.

- Results indicated a high level of mistrust in leadership.

- No actions were taken.

- 6 months later when productivity had declined, the CEO was replaced.

- 3 months later several C-level executives were replaced, none of whom were from HR.

- Productivity and morale continued to slide, and business units were closed.

- 1 year after the original results, the HR director was terminated.

This is an example of leadership that did not see itself and its practices as the cause of the issue. The company's overall results continue to decline.

**Communications company that does not communicate and does not value customers:** in which CxOs step down and earnings decline significantly

*S&P500 telecom company expanded with good intentions.*

- Initial communication reassured customers and employees about job security and positive changes.

*Communication breakdowns began*

- Subsequent direct communication with the customers disappeared leading up to the switch.

*Service and execution failures*

- On transition day, overloaded systems failed, which made service failures for customers the norm and not the exception. Poor communication with employees and customers delayed restoration of service across the affected geographic areas.

*Disastrous customer experiences fueled outrage*

- Company failed to respond to flood of negative social media complaints.

- Company resorted to offering credits to assuage angry customers and problems continued for months

*Summary of the ironic communication and process problems*

- Poor communication within the company hindered service restoration. This also caused undue stress and mistrust for their new, potential "front line" brand ambassadors: their employees.

- Misleading communication with the consumers fueled outrage.

- The complete absence of communication increased negative images of the brand when the company did not respond on social media.

Leadership struggles to explain declining earnings and poor brand image.

# CHANGE C TO COLLABORATE

"I've worked my whole career to be named CxO. Now you want me to collaborate?"

People strive for years to earn a senior level position and aspire to have that coveted C in front of their title. They want to be commanders of their domains. So, why would any leader want to have another department collaborate in their area of expertise? Because it is those very insights, operating in unison, that elevate an organization.

Professional sports teams have a manager or head coach, but every one of them relies on the expertise of their specialists. Depending on the sport, they retain a coach for hitting, pitching, defense, offense et al, and of course scouts, to build the most effective team. Collaboration is essential to building a winning team. Winning teams have more fans and higher revenue.

No single person, not even the CEO, can do everything for a company; that is why there are specialists in every area. Companies serve customers, shareholders, and other stakeholders, not those people assigned to leadership roles. Modern, future-ready leaders must take an insightful, collaborative approach for their organizations.

I have mentored hundreds of college students in various settings. In particular, I have enjoyed being an advisor to the annual business startup competition at my alma mater. Every fall, over 100 teams show up to enter. Only a handful of teams make it through the many required steps to the end. Those finalists present their concepts to the investors for an opportunity to impact their futures. One common factor that keeps teams from advancing to the final round is a lack of ability to execute on their concepts.

At the start of the process, many applicants are engineering students who can build things. Others have brilliant ideas but no way to develop them. All applicants are strongly advised to assemble a team of students and mentors from varied disciplines. They will need members with the combination of skills (i.e. engineering, finance, and marketing) required to take an invention, software, or other solution to the market. Many of the students don't know how to articulate their vision to recruit the specific talent they need to succeed.

In the same way, no one domain "makes" a company. It takes an assemblage of professionals to generate consistent results. In this candidate-driven market, companies are struggling to find and keep the best and brightest minds. Leaders need to build a team that can elevate their companies above the competition and stay there. This takes a strategic eye and a collaborative approach.

## By Design—Lessons on Collaboration from Coca-Cola

Many officers of any C-suite are customer-focused. Sales, marketing, service, communication, security, and others help build the external brand. Some focus internally on infrastructure and the people that make any company run. Many executives do not see or take advantage of the benefit of crossover between domains.

I spoke at an event at the Coca-Cola headquarters and spent two days on their headquarters campus. I was so impressed with the level of attention they gave to their employee engagement. One area seemingly unrelated to employee engagement would be facilities management. When they renovated the campus, they did not stop at the typical carpet and paint refresh that most companies do. They updated the look and feel of the interiors with great intention. They created spaces that were bright and inviting, inspiring collaboration. Scattered around the buildings were small alcoves and breakout rooms with whiteboards and chalkboards. Employees could easily sit together and brainstorm. Intentional facility design was both visually appealing and motivating. Facilities management can have a tremendous impact on employees as well as customers.

Hundreds of thousands of employees comprise the Coca-Cola universe. The communications officer methodically tested ways to unify the disparate employees worldwide.

Leadership prioritizes the impact of their visibility and interaction with the employees. Executives hold town hall meetings at the various locations, so the employees can interact with leadership. The leaders rotate and present topics, answer questions, and interact with employees, thereby fueling engagement.

To help simplify life for the employees, the campus has amenities such as a bank, gym, sundry store, hair salon, and other services. Once they get to work, employees don't have to worry about leaving to take care of day-to-day activities. Not every company has the space or budget to create what Coca-Cola has. Within the constraints of your organization though, how could you make your employees' lives better or easier so that they can do more for you? Do what you can with what you have. Functional amenities are more important than fun.

The impact of Coca-Cola's efforts was clear. Each employee I met genuinely seemed very happy to work there. Over two days I interacted with executives, IT, food service, maintenance, security, and other ambassadors. As a group, their work affirmed their commitment to doing their jobs well. Their demeanor showcased that they enjoyed working there. That is employee engagement in action.

## TAKEAWAYS

- In a candidate-driven market especially, in order to build a team that can elevate the company requires a strategic eye and a collaborative approach.

- Working in tandem, leadership across many domains can create a stronger connection between employees and leadership, and create conditions in which they can thrive with the company.

*Only 11% of Leaders perceive HR to be Antici-pators of company needs. 48% are seen as Partners and 41% are seen as Reactors.*

—DDI Global Leadership Forecast 2018

# EVERY COMPANY NEEDS A CHRO

Reactors are not strategic.

At the end of any professional sports season, there is a strategic restructuring based on the success or failure of that season. Managers are fired and hired, and team owners determine which personnel they need to build the ideal teams for the following season. This reality is often dramatized in film.

In the movie *Moneyball*, a biographical sports film based on the Oakland A's 2002 season, the team general manager, Billy Beane, relied on data and probability in his attempt to build a successful team on a limited budget. In *Trouble with the Curve*, talent scouts relied on both art and science to recruit who they predicted would be the next breakout players.

Postseason, every professional sports organization evaluates revenue and expenses. They review facilities management, infrastructure, tools, technology, promotion, marketing, fan relationships, customer experience, advertising, and tickets sales among other things. But talent is paramount to professional sports success. The challenge is in recruiting and retaining the best players and coaches that their budgets will allow.

For companies, fiscal-year reporting is the "season-end review" that leads to strategic planning. Talent is paramount in business, too; yet, in many organizations, human resources is not perceived as a department that plays an integral strategic role. But the function of HR goes beyond merely partnering with and supporting the existing plans of the CEO and CFO; HR must help anticipate needs.

For the CHROs, or HR leaders who think that this collaborative approach is an attempt to usurp their authority or imply that they are somehow incapable, let me explain why this makes so much sense. In fact, it is their role that gives them unique perspective to see where all other departments intersect with HR. It strengthens their impact by facilitating a more strategic, directorial approach to solving the talent problems companies face today and will tomorrow.

Managing human capital needs of any organization is a monstrous task. The demands of handling payroll, benefits, recruiting, wellness, diversity, and more have grown massively. Unfortunately, the administrative or transactional aspects of HR consume so much time. Little is left to take a wider view of corporate strategy.

Human resources, talent management, people officers: These names have evolved for some companies. But their perceived roles have not. In fact, not all companies designate a CHRO. The stats have improved, but 2018 study results vary greatly about the percentage of leaders that view HR as strategic. In the same DDI/EY study referenced above, they also measured the self-perception of HR, and the results were not much better. HR leaders saw themselves as 21% reactor, 62% partner, and only 17% anticipator. While the numbers differ among studies, the fact remains that HR has room to improve with respect to strategic input.

To do this, HR leaders must expand their vision. When presenting ideas for engagement, they must tie data to results. Otherwise valuable initiatives can be viewed simply as "nice to have" and thus deferred. They must look at the organization from the outside, aside from their critical vantage point within. Data and predictive analytics support sound decision-making for personnel recruiting.

CEOs and CFOs both cite talent as a top priority for years to come. In many industries, shortages of specialized skills are major concerns. But it is both recruitment and retention that matter, especially when the cost of turnover is so high. To be future-ready, companies need strategically minded HR leaders that forecast needs.

This talent shortage is not just a personnel issue. It is a company-wide problem that must be solved. None of these efforts can succeed if a company is rigidly attached to silos.

Virtually every department has potential to impact recruitment and retention. The key is to look at both employee and customer interactions through that lens. By collaborating on key areas, it can free up valuable time and financial resources, and create a more consistent brand inside and out.

Working together the CHRO and other department heads can use relevant analytics to help identify long range needs for skills, as well as plan for up-skilling and cross skilling to support growth. The current methods of seeing HR as the gateway to talent no longer work. By collaborating, leaders can surgically and strategically build the corporate team for the future.

## TAKEAWAYS

- All leaders must be forecasters and embrace impact that people have on recruitment and retention.

- Use past and predictive data along with feedback from employee and customer interactions to anticipate needs.

*84% of the value of the S&P 500
companies is intangible assets.*

—Ocean Tomo Intangible Asset Market Value Study

# OVERCOMING THE 'NICE TO HAVE' LANGUAGE BARRIER

Collaboration and communication require that everyone understands one another.

Each CxO is a specialist in their own realm, communicating with their own corresponding jargon. We are all comfortable speaking to colleagues using our respective vernaculars. However, when our goal is to convince someone outside of our specialty to take action, we need to speak in terms they understand, forecasting outcomes that matter to the other party. While that may seem obvious, this is why many budget proposals do not get approved.

I recently read an open letter from a software company CFO written to their CMO, which illuminated the common language barrier between finance and other departments. Some departments are often considered the revenue spenders instead of the generators. The CFO essentially said to the CMO, don't pitch to me using jargon only you understand. Give me content and data to support your request.

Breaking down silos is a requirement for collaboration. So is breaking down language barriers. Marketing and HR expenses can often seem like they belong in the "nice to have" column of the general ledger. Those department leaders are forced to connect the dots with numbers and data that support their cases.

A few years ago, Oracle released a report that dove deeper into the finding that 84% of the value of the S&P 500 companies was comprised of intangibles. Oracle's research found that the top four value drivers were client relationships, quality of business processes (infrastructure), customer satisfaction, and quality of human capital. These metrics are not always monitored by companies, and even when they are, the proof is not as clearly defined as companies would like. Ironically, human capital is the key to the success or failure of the other value drivers.

For example, there had been a decline in productivity and an increase in discord among employees in the service department of a technology company. The HR director proposed having weekly lunches for the customer service team, as a means of increasing connection among the team members. By supplying the metrics as the driver for the proposal, it was approved. When it was proposed without data, the CFO initially dismissed the idea as a non-essential expense.

HR initiatives often directly correlate to both customer satisfaction and revenue generating results. HR leaders need to think strategically and clearly illustrate the financial gains associated with their proposed budgets. Cost savings should also be highlighted when turnover is reduced through these proactive efforts. When possible, HR should strive to see how the reduced turnover costs can fund any new recruitment marketing or retention efforts.

# HR and Technology go Together Like PB&J

No one wants a jelly sandwich. Or just a peanut butter one. PB&J complement each other. HR and technology do as well, contrary to the concerns about AI eliminating jobs. In fact, since HR and tech are two areas most rapidly impacting business, it's critical for them to work together.

For employees, technology facilitates work. It is a tool. It can provide predictive data and analytics that streamline processes and serve both the company and the customer. Virtually every goal that human resources may have likely has a technology component. Working with the CIO and CTO, HR can help select the tools best aligned with the existing company infrastructure.

Technology should not be seen as a threat to HR, even when AI is projected to eliminate jobs in the future. While AI will impact certain roles in the future, it may likely lead to new roles that have not yet been created. Using predictive data, technology and other departments should proactively collaborate with HR to address their future talent needs and draw from myriad sources of data. Using strong, data-driven strategic insight, the CHRO can advise the

CEO and CFO on matters like the best methods to reskill valuable workers and thereby retain them.

Technology can help HR stay connected with employees regardless of their location. Consistent communication and feedback are practices that engender trust and keep engagement and productivity high. Depending on the size of the enterprise, there are many options for internal communications platforms. The CIO and/or CTO would know which ones would most seamlessly work with existing infrastructures.

For recruiting purposes, technology can increase visibility in the right places to connect with and build a talent pool for future needs. It can also facilitate the candidate experience, weed out non-ideal applicants, and set the tone for the employee experience before it begins. Companies that need to communicate in an omnichannel fashion with candidates to ensure that they are capturing the attention of hard-to-find talent can do so now.

At a recent digital customer experience conference, I previewed comprehensive tools that combined AI, chat, and video to facilitate the sales process and generate impressive results. This was a customer-focused event, but the same platforms can be used to enhance the candidate experience. They can help companies see areas where their applications are being abandoned, taking advantage of machine learning to find out why. This insight can help human resources attract more of the ideal employees they want.

An ordinary human resources—technology collaboration should include many components: addressing hiring goals, developing strategies for getting in front of ideal candidates that may not be looking in the places a company typically posts opportunities, and assessing options for internal promotion and recruiting, or monitoring and addressing negative candidate reviews in social media. Instead of evaluating platforms through the HR lens alone, involve a CIO or CTO who handles vetting and managing the platforms that facilitate the customer journey, as well as improve CX and communication. These experts would then be able to see the correlation between HR's current and future needs and perhaps repurpose the power of employee or customer facing platforms in use. Waiting until the situation is urgent or that needs to be retrofitted is usually not as smooth or cost efficient as a strategic plan. That said, too much data and technology can overwhelm. Platforms that are too robust lead to poor user experiences and can be more costly. Be selective in the technologies you choose to complement your goals.

This includes the internal tools and technology that employees use daily. Ironically companies do not always solicit the insight and critical feedback of those using the platforms before they commit to investing in them. An example would be programs that are cumbersome to use, slow down services and productivity. When employees must create workarounds to execute their workload and meet company metrics this causes friction and increases stress.

The key is to use the power of technology to streamline work and enhance experiences. While some roles will evolve and other will be phased out because of technology, human interaction can never be fully replaced.

## TAKEAWAYS

- Consistent collaboration across various departments helps leverage the powerful insights gained from both technology and people.

- Infrastructure that falls behind your competitors' can drive away both employees and customers, thus stakeholder feedback should be welcomed and solicited for ways to improve.

# BE SILO-FREE FOR SUCCESS

I heard a story about a mother whose house burned down while she was away. Fortunately, she had four talented, proud, children who were independent tradesman: a plumber, a carpenter, a mason, and an electrician. Each one said that they were going to build a new home for their mother on their own and attempted to do so. But each sibling quickly discovered that individually they did not have the skills to completely build a house. And so, the house was never finished.

By nature, talented leaders are often territorial, have high expectations for themselves, and also have the best of intentions. Yet, many plans and initiatives either are never completed, or they proceed so slowly that they become less effective. Speed and agility are requirements for the state of business today. Many projects and goals could be achieved far more quickly if only executives and departments collaborated. However, *when* collaboration begins is equally important to the outcomes.

It is not enough to create the plan and bring in assistance when a particular task falls out of our domain, or when we reach a state of burnout. This also slows progress. Goals are met faster when collaboration is part of the initial plan. A house cannot be built with each tradesman doing their part and then handing it off to the next one. The inner workings of a building must be installed concurrently, not sequentially.

## PEOPLE CONCERNS ARE COMPANY CONCERNS

Very often, executives and departments fail to realize that they should collaborate on a project, especially when the issue seems to be regarding talent or people. None of this is to imply that the CHRO is unqualified or unable to execute their role adequately. CxOs are much stronger and effective when working together strategically and proactively than when working separately or reactively for the organization.

Of course, the most important planning must begin with the CEO, CFO, and CHRO to work tightly together. They must outline how to build and maintain the best team to serve the enterprise goals, not only now but 10 years from now. Executing the plans will require consistent leadership, communication, and financial support, as well as Board buy-in. Expenditures not immediately recognized as priorities may require education. Thus, the Communications Officer must have an integral role in execution and delivery. Plans that are not well communicated falter and often fail.

Silos evolve for many reasons in organizations. Some are intentional, created by territorial sales teams, for example. Or they come as a result of departments or leaders that like to control dissemination of information. Others are unintentional, due to infrastructures and company practices that have been outgrown and impede progress. Silos usually slow business down, often aggravate customers, and cause poor experiences for both customers and employees.

## Scenario—Intentional Silos

A television network has sales offices serving regional markets around the country. An advertiser wants to buy an ad for a time-sensitive event and needs a quote from her account executive for the combined cost for all the markets they need. Due to the territorial siloed sales practices of this network, the advertiser cannot get answers quickly enough because the AE must wait for the various offices to get back to him. The advertiser tells her AE that the other networks can provide the quote immediately, and so they will give the sale to the other networks instead. This network mired in siloed procedures had a history of similar lost revenue due to silos. Lost revenue affects both the network and the commissioned sales people.

## Scenario—Unintentional Silos

How many times have you had to call a customer service representative only to be transferred to another representative where you must repeat your story? This is one of the biggest complaints customers have. Yet so many companies fail to improve. On one call, an agent for one of the largest cosmetics companies explained that she needed me to repeat my situation because the sales department did not have access to the same information as the billing resolution department. She tried to explain that this was for security reasons, but it was a thinly veiled excuse and indicative of the lack of respect that companies have for customers. This negatively impacts revenue, brand image, and strains customer service departments that are forced to work with inferior systems. *Tip:* If you are losing CS agents in your organization, you are also losing customers.

Create a silo-free zone in your strategic planning meetings, and persuade executives to work together toward a common goal using input from all affected department leaders. This streamlines results and eliminates having to create "Band-Aid" solutions that usually cost more than executing a clean, well-considered plan.

## TAKEAWAYS

- Silos in corporate slow progress. There is so much valuable insight that comes from viewing the problem from the perspective of each domain. Too often companies retreat to their departments too soon.

- People concerns are company concerns. Every department is affected and must work together toward solutions.

*84% of happy employees research the company before applying for a job.*

—CareerArc Employer Branding Study

# RECRUITMENT MARKETING, RETENTION, AND RELATIONSHIPS 101

Retention is all about relationships. This applies equally to customers and employees. And while we speak often of the importance of building and maintaining customer relationships, employee relationships are often ignored. But how much do we really know about employee relationships? When does the relationship begin for employees? Many hiring managers may not realize this, but your relationship with your employees begins before they ever meet you. Like your customers, happy employees are discerning.

Just as customers choose to do their research before first contacting a company, employees do the same. They do their homework, read reviews, and look for indications of what it would be like as an employee for a company in which they might be interested. Today's candidates look at a company website and watch employer-brand videos to help determine if they can see themselves working there.

Consider high school students making plans for their futures. When they explore prospective colleges, one of the first tools they use before visiting the schools are the videos that showcase the campus and students. They want to know if they can fit in. Likewise, prospective employees want to know if they fit in with a company.

What does recruitment marketing look like for your organization? Would it attract the best and brightest talent at any level? Would you want to work there based on what you see? And is your brand authentic? Recruitment marketing gets their attention. The candidate process brings them in. Onboarding orients them. In all cases, these processes should be authentic representations of your employer brand. Once new employees start, they should not be surprised by what occurs once they enter the front doors and are escorted to their work space.

There's an old human resources joke I heard years ago, but it is still as relevant as ever. One day, while walking downtown, a human resources exec was struck and tragically killed by a cab. Her soul arrived up in Heaven where she was greeted by Saint Peter.

Saint Peter explained that there was a problem with checking her in. "Oddly we've never once had an HR executive make it this far, and we're really not sure what to do with you." But he told her that she would have to spend one day in Hell and one day in Heaven to decide where she would spend eternity.

The HR manager was sent on an elevator down to Hell. The doors opened and she stepped out onto a beautiful golf course. Standing in front of her were all her friends—fellow HR professionals that she had worked with. They were all dressed in vibrant colors; they hugged her and talked about old times. They played golf, and afterward, at the country club, she enjoyed a surf and turf dinner. She met the Devil, who was surprisingly very nice; they laughed, danced for hours. The HR exec was enjoying herself, and before she knew it, it was time to leave. Everybody shook her hand and waved goodbye as she got onto the elevator. The elevator went up and the door opened at Heaven, where Saint Peter was waiting for her.

It was time for her to spend a day in Heaven. So, the HR manager spent the next 24 hours lounging around on the clouds, playing the harp and singing. It was glorious and peaceful; before she knew it, time was up and Saint Peter came for her.

"So, you've spent a day in Hell and you've spent a day in Heaven. Now you must choose your eternity," he said. The HR exec paused for a second and then replied, "Well, I never thought I'd say this. I mean, Heaven was really great, but I think I had a better time in Hell." So, Saint Peter brought her to the elevator and again the HR exec took the long ride back to Hell.

When the doors of the elevator opened, she found herself standing in a desolate wasteland. She saw that her friends were dressed in rags and were picking up trash and putting it in bags for dinner. The Devil came up to her, put his arm around her, and laughed at her.

"I don't understand," stuttered the HR manager. "Yesterday, when I was here, there was a golf course, a country club; we ate lobster and we danced and had a great time. All there is now is a wasteland of garbage, and all my friends look miserable."

The Devil looked at her and grinned: "That's because yesterday, we were recruiting you… but today you are staff."

Whether companies are selling to customers or employees, they naturally want to put their best image forward. The thrill of landing a new account or hiring a new employee will be short-lived if the brand on the outside does not reflect the reality of the inside.

Culture can be an overwhelming term to embrace. Decide first what you want your employer brand to be. What should it look like to work for your company? Once established, showcase your employer brand throughout the recruiting and hiring process. Promoting your brand means looking for your ideal prospects where they are, not expecting them to come and find you. This must be as intentional as the marketing efforts for your customers. It should be an active campaign to attract the talent pool you want to create and draw from for future roles when they arise.

Once you welcome new hires, there should be consistency throughout the onboarding process about what it means to be a part of your team. It is important for managers to set the conditions for employees to succeed. Reinforce the importance of tying purpose to the mission of the company. New hires thrive and stay when the relationship is nurtured from the outset.

Long-term retention requires ongoing communication to ensure that employees are meeting goals, and that employers are providing the conditions and environment to do so. Cultivating employees, especially in a tight job market, builds brand ambassadors and eases future-readiness.

## TAKEAWAYS

- Today's candidates immediately look for signals in the company employer narrative and videos to see if they could fit in there. Take an honest look at yours.

- Is your recruitment marketing an actual campaign, much like you would pursue customers? If not, it is time to collaborate with marketing, communications and tech.

- New hires should not be surprised by what they find when they become staff. Be authentic and transparent throughout the process.

- If "culture" is too broad a term to tackle in your organization, start with defining your employer brand.

- Remember that employee relationships that must be nurtured to last.

# Stacking Your Team, Talent Shortage or Not

It was a cyclical pattern. No matter how successful or a-ward-winning the previous year's engagement had been, the calls would begin in July. In fact, the more successful the team had been that year, the more that our competition wanted to poach from us. And we always found ourselves facing the same questions: Who was staying on the team? Who wanted a more starring role in the future? Who wanted to move on for political reasons? Who thought they could get a better offer elsewhere? As leaders, we knew the best way to handle the situation was to get out in front before it got out of hand, and potentially lose any top talent.

Fortunately, the team leader excelled at this type of diplomacy. He looked past the posturing because he knew the ultimate goal: ensure the team was stacked with talent. Stressful as it was, recruiting and retaining top talent was an expected part of the process. For us to continue competing and winning at a high level, we needed a deep bench. And, of course, the success of our team also made it easier for us to attract additional high performers. But it was a delicate balance, because too many new stars could drive away current members of the team who felt threatened.

This scenario could probably play out on any number of high-powered sales teams and business units. But in this case, it was stacking a team of highly competitive youth travel softball players. Regardless of how experienced or successful coaches had been, future success was contingent on having the right talent consistently on their teams. Leaders lead and develop teams, but the players execute; so, having a strategic combination of skills in each position was essential. Travel softball coaches need strong pitching, key defensive position players, and a dynamic offense that work together.

In business, the same truths exist. No matter how qualified are CEOs or leaders, they cannot meet and exceed goals without a stacked team.

Talent is a priority for CEOs, CFOs, and organizations, according to virtually every current executive survey and study. It is a candidate's market right now and jobs are plentiful. Yet many companies are not finding and retaining the skilled people they want and need in their organizations.

When your sales team promotes your products or services, do your marketing materials, website, trade show displays, social media presence, infrastructure, and locations say, "we're average... but come buy from us anyway?" Or, do they proclaim, "we're the solution to your problem, the service you need, the product you love to buy, over and over again?"

If your goal is mediocrity, then the first approach may work as you keep replacing your one-time customers.

But if your goal is to be best-in-class and dominate your market, your intent should be to do everything possible to project that image out into the market place. You know who your ideal client is. You know their needs and can communicate in all the right ways to build relationships and deliver an outstanding customer experience. And, of course, your products and services deliver on those promises so that customers remain loyal.

Can you say, though, that you put equal effort, attention, and investment into the recruiting and retention of the employees needed to produce those best-in-class goods for your customers, and deliver for your shareholders? If you are like most companies and executives, you do not.

For a long time, companies got away with being average in respect to their employee relationships. Why? Because they could. There were ample supplies of quality applicants and candidates to supplement or replace employees. Technology had not disrupted the way people find jobs, exposed working conditions, or changed employee expectations forever.

Stacking your team should be a priority across the enterprise. Just as companies understand, plan, and invest in the lifecycle of the customer journey, they must understand and actively recruit wide candidate pools to serve future enterprise needs and succession plans. Employers must then invest, nurture, and keep these valued assets.

Much like companies strategically target customers, they must do the same for employees. When specialized skills are needed, the search must be more precise. If a specific role or person is in high demand, it is critical to look for those people where they are, not where you want them to find your job postings. Successful sales people use customer avatars to find more ideal clients. Employers must use similar tactics to identify ideal candidates and pursue them in their natural environments.

This is not a human resources function to determine who and where the targeted pool may be. It takes a leadership team approach to build and keep a future-ready organizational team.

## TAKEAWAYS

- Evaluate the level of effort, attention, and investment you currently have in marketing to attract and retain the employees needed to consistently produce your best-in-class goods and services.

- The evergreen supply of applicants is gone. Companies must get proactive and creative to attract prospects, so you can adequately stack your team.

# AGILE COMPANIES CANNOT BE FLAT-FOOTED

"Don't get caught flat-footed." Any athlete who has heard that phrase knows that it means be in a ready-stance. To be able to move in the direction of a play at all times you should be on the balls of your feet. That allows a player to "read" how the ball is coming off a baseball bat, or over a net, or off a backboard, so that you can react and make the best possible play. It means being agile, nimble and ready to go in any direction. To stand flat-footed means you cannot react quickly enough to execute.

In corporate the same principle applies. If you are flat-footed you are not well prepared for planned competition or unplanned situations. It may seem simplistic, but scenarios catch companies off guard because they are unaware, unprepared or not positioned to move quickly. The result is that either they lose to the competition or they cannot adapt and react quickly enough to a situation or opportunity to capitalize on it.

Addressing this talent situation is one of those circumstances. Being flat-footed and looking for people to fill roles as you need them will not help create wins. Agility allows for taking a strategic approach to create a pool of talent ready to draw from when opportunities arise.

We began this book talking about competition. One of the competitive challenges all companies face is with keeping up with rising payroll costs. While fair pay is still the main consideration for employees of all ages, it is not the only factor. Your organization should of course know and keep pace with the salary benchmarks for roles in your industry. However, it should also take a nimble approach to providing what employees want beyond the paycheck and benefits. People want work-life balance and flexibility. They want career advancement training and opportunities. They want an appealing physical work environment.

Companies must keep a pulse on what is important to their workforce. If they communicate with them regularly this should be easy. Even when it is not possible to match the financial offer of a competitor, creating offers that appeal to employee priorities can help you keep and add key talent.

*85% of the jobs projected for 2030 have not yet been invented.*

—Institute for the Future (IFTF) & Dell Technologies

## LIFETIME LEARNING AND DEVELOPMENT: INVEST IN YOUR FUTURE

It is difficult but not impossible to plan for roles that have yet to be imagined. And while these roles of the future may not exist, you can prepare in advance if you have a pool of employees with core skills and qualities that can be shaped to fill these impending positions.

Whenever I meet very young athletes and I ask them what positions they play on a team, I can tell how they have been coached by their answers. The ones who will become more valuable players later on usually reply: I am a lacrosse player, or a baseball player… not a midfielder or a shortstop. When we coached our softball teams at their youngest ages, we taught them to know all the positions, so they could play interchangeably. In that way, they learned the game from all vantage points, not from one position only. Even pitchers and catchers learned to play other positions.

College softball coaches recruit players that can fill key roles. But they also recruit and appreciate versatility because the unexpected can happen. A player may get injured, transfer, or is just not performing well. The most versatile players have two strong qualities: They have the general knowledge and skills to step into multiple roles, and they have the attitude to do so for the good of the team.

Of course, companies need specialists in key roles. But they need employees with open minds and a commitment to the brand's mission. That is why cultivating that philosophy is so important. As roles are projected to evolve, companies can plan accordingly with the high potential talent they have. Provide them the opportunities to train and grow with and for the organization.

Some leadership and board members may have concerns that their companies will invest in employees that may ultimately leave. This is the wrong mindset and sets up an expectation for failure. If the employer brand and culture are strong and you are giving employees reasons to stay, the risk is worth taking. Stay connected with your employees and nurture their expectancy for the future.

Recruit strong employees that you can move into roles as they become needed. Learning platforms and skills training options abound in every industry. Selecting the best for your organization requires input and collaboration from many angles. If there is an L&D Officer, they need direction from the CEO, CFO, and CHRO for what roles maintain and elevate employees. Technology Officers can identify which platforms work best with the infrastructure. Communicating the value of optional training is key to attracting participants. Employees in whom the company invests should understand the necessity of a mutual level of commitment to the future.

Training and development enable companies to take a proactive stance instead of being reactive to market conditions.

## TAKEAWAY

Leaders who are reluctant to invest, for fear that employees will leave with their new skills, sets up an expectation for failure. If the employer brand and culture are strong and you are giving employees reasons to stay, the risk is worth taking.

# RECRUITING MILLENNIAL AND GEN Z EMPLOYEES

Baby boomers, Gen Xers, millennials, Gen Zers, and all forms of cultural and gender diversity comprise the workforce of businesses today.

For companies that cannot understand how their job posts are not attracting enough candidates or the type of talent they seek, it is time to look inward.

Some companies' recruiting has become antiquated and out of touch with the expectations of today's market. Some are still using practices they used in the 80s and 90s, which will not work on today's employees. To find diverse candidates, hiring managers must search for them where they are and not expect them to seek out their companies.

Companies must invest in current methods, visuals, and technologies that can help increase visibility. For companies that have a high volume of positions to fill and many applicants for each, it may be time to consider AI and other machine-learning options. These alternatives have the dual benefit of freeing up valuable HR time, as well as resources, to hone in on the ideal candidates from the pool. They also accelerate the process for the applicants, who look for instantaneous responses.

This need for speed is another byproduct and attribute of these new generations of employees who, because of technology, seek and expect immediate answers, as well as feedback on their performance. Adapting to expectations of these new cultures impacts hiring results.

Companies that do not hire in high volume can also benefit from the speed, consistency, and visibility that job posting sites offer. Technology can help improve the candidate experience, and this is where HR should enlist the aid of the CTO and CIO to help them vet the best platforms for working with the existing tech and tools in the organization.

If you're hiring millennials or Gen Z employees, they have different values, expectations, and approaches to job searching. These younger cultures were brought up sharing their lives with each other in public view. They have been posting their day-to-day activities in real time via social media, and this is their accepted behavior. If they have poor candidate experiences, they will publicly share their experiences. They will comment about the speed, or lack thereof, of the hiring process. They will reveal poor practices regarding hiring, onboarding, or working in the environment, if these procedures do not reflect the brand with which they thought they were agreeing to partner.

Negative comments and reviews may be seen by the general public, but these individuals' own social media networks will further expose and amplify their opinions about a brand. And, this can adversely affect a brand in the future for potential applicants and for potential customers.

Once hired, the experience and environment that candidates see once they walk through the door on the first day must match what was marketed to them during the hiring process.

Companies must adapt to the changing needs and expectations of new and future generations. At the same time, they must consider the needs of the legacy employees that have taken them to this point. Employees of all generations and cultures should be encouraged to mentor one another, working together to learn from each other, sharing their unique strengths that benefit the entire organization.

## TAKEAWAYS

- Leverage the power of AI, machine learning and other technology that can accelerate the applicant process. This reduces the workload for HR as well as providing the immediate responses today's impatient candidates want.

- Be conscious of your employer image, as poor candidate experiences quickly become public and can impact hiring success rates.

*91% of employers believe a poor "star" rating can win or lose a job applicant.*

—CareerArc Employer Branding Study

## POOR EMPLOYER REVIEWS: DOES YOUR CANDIDATE EXPERIENCE RATE A 1 STAR OR 5 STAR?

Be honest. Does your outward-facing customer brand match your inward-facing employer brand?

It's important for companies to realize that every experience exposed and shared through social media can affect your bottom line. It's not just prospective employees you can repel with a poor candidate experience. The image your customers have of your company is negatively impacted when the candidate or employee experience is poor. Customers want to engage with companies that are honest and treat their employees well.

Before Glassdoor, ZipRecruiter, and Indeed, few, if any, employer reviews or comments about companies or managers were publicly available. Now those sites are the first place that candidates look to determine if they should apply for jobs. Negative employee reviews are preserved and on display like dirty laundry. It astounds me how many companies do not pay attention to these comments and address them, as these companies run the risk of driving away prospects.

Where I lived in the late 1980s, the hot place to go for a burger, drinks and dancing was a 1950s-themed restaurant. The place was retro and hip, and it had wide appeal, attracting people ranging in age from their early 20s, like me, to 50-somethings. Maybe it was the gleaming '57 Chevy that jutted out above the bar as the focal point in each location, or the glitzy chrome and neon. Or the fact that it was pure fun when the staff stopped to dance on top of the bar for certain songs. But the three original locations were packed Thursday through Sunday nights, where people would eat, drink, and dance.

So, when I interviewed for a job as a marketing manager for a new location they recently opened in another part of the state, I was excited. I met with the corporate marketing director and the restaurant manager inside the club, which looked like a Hollywood set even during the daytime. Who wouldn't want to work in such a fun environment? When I got the job and they told me to report for work the following Monday, I couldn't wait to start.

When I arrived, I was greeted by my new boss. She took me from the sleek front of the house, through the kitchen, to a generic-looking wooden door which led to the offices. She opened the door and led me up a dim staircase to a windowless room. The office was small, with worn, shabby furniture and cheap-looking sales flyers stacked on cramped desks. I felt like I had just seen behind the curtain of the Wizard of Oz. I was disappointed and confused; I could not believe this was their office. It got worse within the first week when I learned the truth about the location. They underestimated the fact that this commuter town demographic was not like the other locations. And they didn't have much of a budget left for promotion. Had Glassdoor or Indeed existed, I would have known how bad it was on the inside and never would have applied there.

The bad news is that many companies ignore or disregard the impact of such reviews. So many of them go unaddressed from anyone in HR or leadership. Yes, you will find occasional hater reviews like you might see about a hotel on TripAdvisor or Yelp. But when there is a pattern on employment sites of similar comments about the culture, a particular location, or management, that's a problem.

The good news for proactive companies is that these reviews, however negative, are a roadmap for action. They enable companies to take the information, investigate, and act upon it. If poor reviews are ignored, they can repel prospects. Would you stay in a hotel that had multiple comments about bed bugs? Not only would you avoid the hotel as a customer, you would never apply to work there. Similarly, negative employer reviews repel customers. Customers expect to buy from companies that are socially responsible and judge the character of a brand that does not treat employees well.

Investors want and expect the same from their companies. Internally, if there are policies and procedures that are not being communicated well, they can cause legal concerns. Added costs and negative publicity tarnish brand image, which investors will not tolerate.

## TAKEAWAYS

- Customers want to engage with companies that are honest and treat their employees well.

- Do not dismiss or discount the impact of negative reviews on your ability to recruit and hire or to satisfy investors.

- Periodically evaluate your candidate experience, and take action where indicated.

*Companies cannot find the talent they need. Nearly a third of employers cite a lack of applicants, 20% say candidates lack the experience*

—KPMG U.S. CEO Outlook 2017

# IN CLOSING:
# TEAMWORK IS OF THE UTMOST IMPORTANCE

*Houston, we have a problem.*

When the Apollo 13 astronauts made that fateful statement, my friend's father was one of the NASA engineers called in to solve the problem. Imagine being presented with that challenge. This team of engineers was in uncharted territory and had to think out of the box to literally save lives, drawing on the expertise and problem-solving skills of each engineer. That team worked tirelessly, under pressure to create the best possible conditions for the astronauts to return. In that moment, NASA had to work with the people that they had and the tools and technology available. They did not have the luxury of waiting for additional time, equipment, or manpower. They didn't need to, however;

they had recruited exceptionally well, and that team rose to the challenge.

Companies today may not always have the best talent in house for current, future, or unplanned needs. They must first recruit well, not adequately. Second, they must have the ability to cultivate from within, as well as have a pool of "warm" talent from which to draw when needs arise. When critical situations occur, or when companies must simply keep productivity high, having a team that is committed to the same purpose and mission is essential.

The evolution of business will only increase in momentum, and companies must be ready to adapt and grow to meet the needs of customers. The increased demands on business and the need to create a competitive edge cannot happen without strong people to execute on those needs.

Market conditions now favor candidates and will for the foreseeable future. When companies need workers with specific skills and risk losing them to competitors, they must think creatively about how to find and keep their most valuable assets. The recruitment marketing and retention strategies that worked before are insufficient now.

Prospects will not come looking for jobs in the same ways they did before. Candidates have expectations for how the interview process should go. And those who are in high demand have options, so time is critical. Candidates also have expectations for the hiring and onboarding experiences. Employees want to feel that they are a part of a larger mission and that their work has value. They want more than a paycheck and traditional benefits. They want flexibility, work-life balance, and transparency, among other things. When candidates' expectations don't align with the company's reality, then they share these experiences with others. For younger workers, sharing on social media is in their nature, which can have positive or negative consequences. Again, individual, disgruntled comments are not concerning, but overall negative commentary is. They have the potential to harm revenue, the customer brand experience, the employer brand, and therefore, investor relations.

The top three human strengths that employers value the most are verbal and written communication, collaboration, and problem-solving skills (Manpower Group Talent Shortage Survey 2018). Excellent communication is needed to collaborate and work toward a common solution. It makes perfect sense, then, that the C-suite would collaborate on a challenge as complex as the talent shortage.

Recently, there was a dramatic rescue mission to save 12 young Thai soccer players and their coach. While exploring a cave in Thailand, they found themselves trapped 2.5 miles inside the cave for over two weeks without food or supplies, as a result of monsoon rain flooding. Conditions rapidly deteriorated. The only way out was by undertaking a treacherous sequence of scuba dives through dark, narrow passages. The alternative was to wait inside the isolated cave for four months until monsoon season waters would recede. Thai Navy SEALs and divers from around the world came together to rescue these players and their coach. These highly experienced divers and engineers worked together along side international teams that they had never met prior to being thrust into this situation.

Requisite to the mission's successful outcome were teamwork, communication, collaboration, and extreme problem-solving skills, not to mention bravery of the highest level. This is another illustration of teamwork at its best.

Of course, a talent shortage is not life threatening. It is a costly challenge and a high priority for many companies though. The challenge of addressing a complex problem, especially under poor conditions, can be overcome faster by communicating and working together. In the rescue examples above, the focus was on the outcome: saving lives. Companies often mistakenly weaken their outcomes by immediately going to the departmental silos to execute steps, instead of identifying the overall goal and confronting it from many angles to solve it together.

Generally speaking, companies strive to beat earnings estimates by exceeding customer expectations with the best products, customer service, and overall experience. This requires that the workforce, infrastructure, and essential production capabilities are sufficient enough to deliver on those promises. People are the key to success and often are the differentiator in a crowded market.

Stacking your team with the best possible players is not the sole responsibility of human resources. What makes up a company's employer reputation—what it means to work inside the company—requires infrastructure, facilities, communication, mission, morale, learning, opportunities for growth, and strong management. All of these, and more, compel the human resources department to find, attract, and hire the best candidates. This is your employer brand, and it requires the participation and support of all leaders and their departments to create an environment that attracts the type of talent needed to deliver on company goals. Without that, it is akin to driving with your foot on the brake.

Leaders who can collaborate on the common goals of finding, attracting, and retaining the best employees will help the company maximize revenue, retention, and loyalty for the long term.

For companies that recruit well, the team you have can carry you further than you think. Remove silos and create conditions for success. Cultivate skills and nurture the relationships you have with your existing team, to ensure that they stay with you. Vitalize them to the shared mission to deliver for customers. Leverage the skills, technology, and knowledge you have now to help you find the outside insight and solutions that you will need to create lasting change.

It will take strong leadership and especially the collaboration of the CEO, CFO, CHRO, and CCO. It will also take the expertise of the rest of the C-suite's problem-solving skills and insights. The value and impact of effective and authentic communication cannot be overstated. Determine how to better market the company as an employer brand as much you do as a customer brand. Seek outside help and ideal insight to address your organization's unique challenges. Listen, communicate, and use feedback as a guide.

But time is of the essence. Top talent is in short supply and today's candidates have options. Become the employer brand that keeps the people you have and attracts those you need for growth.

Attracting and keeping talent is a team sport. Collaborate, communicate, create change.

It is time to work together.

# SECTION THREE
## WORKSHEETS

# How to use these worksheets

The most difficult step in any endeavor is usually the first one: acknowledging that things could be better, or should at least be assessed. What follows that objective assessment is determining the best place or way to begin to make changes. These worksheets are a very basic outline of many topics covered in the book. They are designed to get you thinking about how:

- your leaders could be more collaborative,

- they are communicating now,

- situations are currently perceived, and

- the organization can take a more proactive approach to the talent issues they face.

Use them as a place to gain perspective and start discussions that lead to creating lasting change.

**COLLABORATION** WORKSHEET $\boxed{A}$

Take a strategic view and work backwards from the goal or the problem.
Goal/Problem _____

Cost if not addressed_____

Departments affected _____

Personnel roles that you do <u>not</u> have but need to achieve the goal:
_____
_____

Technology that you do <u>not</u> have but need to achieve the goal.
_____
Existing Tech that can be leveraged _____

Skills training needed to achieve the goal:
_____
_____

Set 6 Month Action Steps

| 30 Days | 60 Days | 90 Days | 180 Days |
|---------|---------|---------|----------|
|         |         |         |          |

How can a communication strategy help ensure better outcomes?
_____
_____

Roles that should collaborate on the goal/problem:
☐ CEO          ☐ CFO          ☐ CHRO          ☐ CCO
☐ CxO_____  ☐ CxO_____  ☐ CxO_____   ☐ CxO_____

**INTROSPECTION** WORKSHEET

Do your customer brand and employer brand match? _____
If not, where must they change?
_____
_____

Does your organization actively promote its employer brand? _____ If so, how:
☐ Company website _____
☐ Via social media _____
☐ Employer brand/culture videos _____
☐ Via channels of interest to prospects _____
If not, why not? _____

Do you regularly (at least 2x per year) survey and communicate with employees?
If not, why not?
☐ Too many technology options       ☐ Gaining approval
☐ Not knowing where to start         ☐ We don't follow through post-survey

On your last survey, what results surprised you the most?
_____
_____

How are survey concerns addressed? (via HR alone or with other departments?
_____
_____

Has communication or trust in leadership been a concern from employees? _____
If yes, describe actions taken to address it:
_____
_____

Roles that should collaborate on the goal/problem:
☐ CEO            ☐ CFO            ☐ CHRO            ☐ CCO
☐ CxO_____     ☐ CxO_____     ☐ CxO_____     ☐ CxO_____

**MISSION & PURPOSE** WORKSHEET

C

Does the company have a mission statement that makes sense with the <u>current</u> conditions, values and goals of the company? _____

Define it here: _____
_____
_____

Do all employees know what that mission is? _____
How do you know and monitor this? _____

Do they know how their specific role fits into the success of the mission? _____
How do you measure this? _____

Do managers reiterate and reinforce this in their regular interactions with employees?
How? _____

Do leaders take an active role in this philosophy? _____
It cannot be a "set it and forget it" approach. It must be a set the example approach.
These are all questions that should be corroborated in surveys.
How could leaders do a better job of communicating this philosophy? _____
_____
_____

*Remember that companies that tie mission to purpose for the employees have greater productivity and outperform competitors by up to 42%.*

If employees were asked if they "have" to go to work, or if they "want" to be at work, how would they answer?_____
Why, and how you could improve that? _____
_____
_____

List the tools that you use for employee communication and motivation:
_____
_____

Roles that should collaborate on the goal/problem:
☐ CEO          ☐ CFO          ☐ CHRO          ☐ CCO
☐ CxO_____  ☐ CxO_____  ☐ CxO_____   ☐ CxO_____

**RECRUITING PRACTICES** WORKSHEET

When departments need new hires, who writes the job description?
☐ HR    ☐ Department supervisor    ☐ Use previous ones ☐ Google it

What percentage of applicants do not meet expectations?
☐ 10%  ☐ 25%  ☐ 50% or more

Compared with 2 years ago, has the average length of time to fill a position
☐ Increased        ☐ Same        ☐ Decreased

Do you monitor the candidate experience and survey those who apply during/after the process? If not, why not? _____
If yes, what feedback have you received? _____
How have you acted upon the feedback? _____
_____

Compared with 5 years ago, is the caliber of college recruit applicants:
☐ Better        ☐ Same        ☐ Worse
If worse, describe the pattern _____
_____
Do you collaborate with the universities to improve results?_____

Recommendation: Work with organizations that are facilitating recruiting such as:

American Corporate Partners which eases the transition from the military to the civilian workforce          https://www.acp-usa.org/

The Mike Rowe Works Foundation which works to educate and close the skills gap with their campaign:          http://profoundlydisconnected.com

Veterans organizations that help pair military veterans with corporate mentors
                    https://acp-advisornet.org

A personal opinion - Military veterans and athletes are usually candidates with a strong work ethic and good time management skills.

Roles that should collaborate on the goal/problem:
☐ CEO          ☐ CFO          ☐ CHRO          ☐ CCO
☐ CxO_____ ☐ CxO_____ ☐ CxO_____ ☐ CxO_____

## GLASSDOOR/INDEED REVIEWS WORKSHEET

Look for patterns in the comments.
Do not dismiss patterns as haters or disgruntled employees.

Applicants look for patterns in the responses too. Take care not to sound disingenuous. Respond to comments authentically or not at all. For example if prospects see responses that all sound like this:
"We are sorry that you feel...." It sounds like the writer is implying it is the fault of the commenter.
Value the comments that indicate trends as they are a way to correct problems and create change.

Do you monitor the employment social media sites for feedback? Regardless of your role in leadership, this should be a habit.
If not, why not? _____
_____

Are your company's responses
authentic?_____

Look for patterns. Are any of the comments recurring about:
☐ Leadership      ☐ Communication      ☐ Period of time _____
☐ Departments _____
☐ Locations _____
☐ Positions _____

Action steps:
Use this insight as a way to investigate problems and take corrective steps if/where necessary.
Use comments about leadership, communication and other issues to support your budgetary proposals for corrective measures.
Compare your overall company presence, including descriptions and videos with competitors. Note any differences.
_____
_____

Roles that should collaborate on the goal/problem:
☐ CEO            ☐ CFO            ☐ CHRO            ☐ CCO
☐ CxO_____  ☐ CxO_____  ☐ CxO_____    ☐ CxO_____

## CORPORATE RESTRUCTURING WORKSHEET

F

Planning for Announcing the Restructuring, Merger, Acquisition, et al.

If you are a team, you must weather changes together. No one likes change, but when people feel blindsided by a last minute announcement, they naturally wonder if they can trust the leaders that kept them in the dark about plans that will most definitely affect them.

Work backward from the effective date. Part of the planning that leadership does must include a strong communications plan. Create messages for all affected stakeholders, with attention to the concerns on how that group will be affected and what roles they will play. Media and customer announcements must be planned as needed.

| | Leadership | Managers | Employees | Investors |
|---|---|---|---|---|
| **30** D A Y S | | | | |
| **60** D A Y S | | | | |
| **90** D A Y S | | | | |
| **180** D A Y S | | | | |

Roles that should collaborate on the goal/problem:

☐ CEO          ☐ CFO          ☐ CHRO          ☐ CCO
☐ CxO_____  ☐ CxO_____  ☐ CxO_____   ☐ CxO_____

t

**COMMUNICATION & LEADERSHIP** WORKSHEET   G

Leaders can increase the respect and trust of employees when they treat them as stakeholders in the operation. The "because leadership said so" approach with no explanation or elaboration lacks the transparency employees want from leaders. Even in difficult times, companies must trust in their employees and convey a plan for the future. If not, they risk voluntary turnover and worse, negative reviews that will impede future hiring.

Leaders, evaluate a time when a message was <u>not</u> received well by employees. Exercise:
• Consider the message, impact, and perspective of the receivers: M-I-P
**Message:** The information to be shared about the situation

_____

_____

**Impact:** The intended outcome from sharing the message: What is the goal?

_____

_____

**Perspective:** Anticipate how the message will be received in its current form. If it could be negatively perceived, repeat the process to proactively address any objections. Consider the receiver's perspective and connect that to the common goal for better outcomes. _____

_____

_____

How could it have been handled differently for better outcomes?

_____

_____

What tools or technology may have improved delivery or employee response?

_____

_____

Roles that should collaborate on the goal/problem:
☐ CEO ☐ CFO ☐ CHRO ☐ CCO
☐ CxO_____ ☐ CxO_____ ☐ CxO_____ ☐ CxO_____

**CHANGING BEHAVIORS** WORKSHEET

New initiatives, updated policies, upgrades to infrastructure, compliance issues, and correcting unacceptable conduct: All of these actions and more demand that we change our behaviors. This can happen more readily when the change is *inspired* not commanded.

ACTION STEPS

• Identify the goal and what needs to change to achieve it.

_____
_____

• Gain leadership buy-in across the enterprise and within departments as it applies.

_____
_____

• Leadership must set the example. Caution: When leaders take set-it-and-forget-it approaches, or if they feel that a single statement or announcement will suffice to change behaviors, their efforts cannot succeed. *How can you expect employees to follow leads that fizzle? What tools can leaders use to support the initiative?*

_____
_____

• Set the conditions and provide the tools and technology that help create new behaviors. List those here:

_____
_____

• Reward early adopters to entice more ambassadors. What rewards work best in your organization?

_____
_____

• Use tools and technology to help employees embrace the messages. Brainstorm:

_____
_____

Roles that should collaborate on the goal/problem:
☐ CEO          ☐ CFO          ☐ CHRO          ☐ CCO
☐ CxO_____  ☐ CxO_____  ☐ CxO_____   ☐ CxO_____

A simple illustrative tool to show how any domain's plans include personnel and technology, and thereby an opportunity to collaborate with those (and other) departments to ensure best outcomes. Silos impede progress. Work toward goals together.

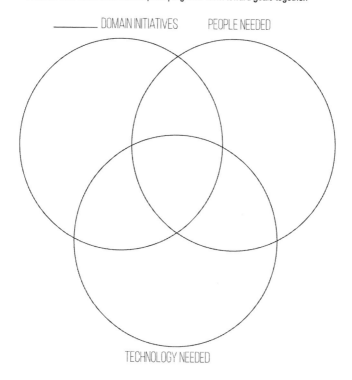

_____ DOMAIN INITIATIVES       PEOPLE NEEDED

TECHNOLOGY NEEDED

Roles that should collaborate on the goal/problem:
☐ CEO          ☐ CFO          ☐ CHRO          ☐ CCO
☐ CxO_____ ☐ CxO_____ ☐ CxO_____ ☐ CxO_____

**GENERAL COUNSEL/ LEGAL** WORKSHEET

The General Counsel is a key to illuminating the areas that must change. Human resources must inform and establish policies. Communications can help ensure that messaging is relevant and "sticks" with employees. The CIO facilitates the delivery of the message via company infrastructure. Leaders from all domains must:
 a) support these changes, b) lead by example, and c) enforce policies
Note: Poor communication, poor company culture, or a damaged employer brand may also stem from a lack of emotional intelligence from managers.

**Common internal legal matters:** (i.e. ageism, sexual harassment, et al)

_____
_____
_____
_____

**Brainstorm preventative measures that could mitigate such matters:** (i.e. clearer policies, stronger enforcement of policies, consistent management styles, et al)

_____
_____
_____
_____

**Communication's role in delivering the above:**

_____
_____
_____
_____

**Technology needed:**

_____
_____
_____
_____

**Leadership or other Training needed:**

_____
_____
_____
_____

Roles that should collaborate on the goal/problem:
- ☐ CEO
- ☐ CFO
- ☐ CHRO
- ☐ CCO
- ☐ CxO_____
- ☐ CxO_____
- ☐ CxO_____
- ☐ CxO_____

# Acknowledgements

I live my life as a team sport, as we are only as good as those we surround ourselves with. Thank you to all of my teams. In particular I would like to acknowledge some key players.

First, and foremost my Family.

I have dedicated this book to my wonderful parents, who have taught us the importance of love and family. And I adore mine.

To the love of my life, Eric, thank you for being everything that a best friend and partner could be. You bring out the best in me, make me laugh every day and I can't imagine my life without you. To my stepdaughters Tori and Sam, thank you for sharing your lives with me. I love you and am so proud of you, now and for what you will accomplish in the future.

To my brother Joe and "sister" Jessica, I love and admire you both so much and am grateful that I have family that I call friends too. To my nieces Olivia and Mia, keep following your passions. You are both going to do great things in life and I will be cheering you on as you do. I am thankful, proud of you and love being your aunt.

## My Business Team

I am humbled and fortunate to have had very long standing relationships with so many clients. None of that client trust and support can happen without a strong core team to serve them. I would especially like to thank Meg, for your loyalty and your above and beyond commitment to our clients' success. Shadra and Dave, thank you for strategically amplifying my voice, visibility and reach as only you can.

For 30-plus years, I have had the privilege of being a trusted advisor to a cohort of elite executive clients. Thank you all.

# About the Author

A change agent and trusted advisor to the C-suite for decades, Denise Graziano helps companies differentiate and gain competitive advantage in their market, by leveraging the power of positive employee and customer experiences.

Companies and high-level leaders often don't realize the challenges and impressions they're presenting to their team members and customers. Miscommunication, lack of clarity, and feedback not being heard, valued, or understood can start to erode productivity and trust. Denise helps companies see how their interactions internally with employees and externally with customers could be sabotaging their growth and how to correct it.

Denise Graziano is a leading authority in helping mid-market companies to improve trust, relationships and communication inside their organization with employees and externally with clients to increase revenue, retention and loyalty. A strategic thinker and leader with over 30 years of business experience, Denise is a speaker and author of Talent is a Team Sport.

She is CEO of Graziano Associates, a boutique marketing communications firm with a unique internal and external approach that helps companies to vitalize their workforce, and build brand ambassadorship from within.

* * *

## CONNECT WITH ME:

Website:     grazianoassoc.com
Twitter:     @grazianoassoc
Facebook:    facebook.com/GrazianoAssoc/
LinkedIn:    linkedin.com/in/denisemgraziano
Blog:        grazianoassoc.com/news-blog/

# Thank you for reading my book.

If you have been inspired by *Talent is a Team Sport*, please pass it along or give it as a gift to another leader who may benefit from these perspectives on how to help address their talent concerns.

I would be extremely grateful if you could leave a quick review on Amazon. Your reviews and recommendations to colleagues are essential for me to spread the message and help other leaders who are eager to make strategic changes to their organizations. Thank you in advance for your support.

Finally, get in touch! If I may be a resource you in the future, let's talk. Email me at: denise@grazianoassoc.com.

To your continued success,

Denise Graziano

# DOWNLOAD THE
# WORKSHEETS FREE!

## READ THIS FIRST

Just to say thanks for buying my book, I would like to
give you the worksheets as a full size PDF 100% free

## TO DOWNLOAD GO TO:

http://talentisateamsport.com/worksheets